From aunt _July 2005_

D0728694

Another Place at the Table:

My Mother's Story

Best wishes to Nathalie from the Bologna Lady Mary Cook

by Mary Cook

Published by
Creative Bound Inc.
P.O. Box 424
Carp, Ontario K0A 1L0

(613) 831-3641

ISBN 0-921165-57-9
Printed and bound in Canada

© **1998 Mary Cook**
All rights reserved. No part of this publication may be reproduced, stored in a retrieval system, or transmitted in any form or by any means, electronic, mechanical, photocopying, recording, or otherwise, except for brief quotations used for purposes of review, without the prior written permission of the Publisher.

Book design: Wendelina O'Keefe
Photos supplied courtesy of Mary Cook, Audrey (Haneman) Bergeron, Emerson Haneman, and Ilene and Leo Thom.

About the cover: Born and raised in Ottawa, **Brock Nicol** has been drawing and painting since he was eight years old, and has been a self-employed illustrator since 1987. This cover is his latest collaboration with communications designer Wendelina O'Keefe. Brock's original illustrations also grace the covers of Mary Cook's *Liar, Liar, Pants on Fire!* and *Christmas with Mary Cook*, both published by Creative Bound.

Canadian Cataloguing in Publication Data
Cook, Mary, date
      Another place at the table : my mother's story
ISBN 0-921165-57-9

     I. Title.

PS8555.O566A76 1998   C813'.54   C98-901350-2
PR9199.3.C66A66 1998

This is a work of fiction. It is, however, based on the very real life of Mabel Ernestine Haneman née Lapointe (1898-1971). At the core of this story lies truth, based on my mother's diaries and my childhood recollections.

Dedication

I know, without a doubt, had not the Second World War intervened, and robbed him of six years of his life while he was not much more than a boy, my brother Emerson would have gone on to great heights in the world of design or some other branch of graphics. His love of drawing and inventing has never left him, however. He has gone on to be a vital contributing member of his community and inspired many around him, leaving in his wake a zest for life and a keen sense of loyalty. This book would not have been possible without his encouragement and input, and so this biography of our mother is lovingly dedicated to my brother, Emerson.

Prologue

Mabs was always amazed at the surge of energy she was able to muster when the task at hand was one she relished. It had taken most of the previous day to lug all the furniture out of the log house and stack it in the backyard. She couldn't depend on Albert to be of much help; he thought every last stick should be taken to the new house in town. They would be on their way there within the hour.

Two spool beds formed the base of the pile, and then came the back-to-the-wall cupboard (ugly as sin, Mabs thought) which held next to nothing. A clutch of chairs sat rakishly atop a dough box and a deacon's bench. The bench had spent the last ten years propped against the outside wall at the back door, but Albert never had gotten around to fixing the end leg. Wads of the *Renfrew Mercury* had been stuffed into every crevice of the pyre, waiting for Mabs' match.

Albert stood with his back against a young tree, with his shoulder blades pressed into the trunk. He had planted it four years ago and already it was taller than he was, which wasn't much of a feat when you considered Albert stood 5' 6" in his work socks. He turned ever so slightly, so that his eyes didn't have to look at the mound of furniture he had known for his entire life. Eleven-year-old Mary, scrawny as a young plucked chicken, played a final game of jacks on the pump platform before tucking the drawstring sack into the bookbag she would use as a carry-all on the trip into town. Audrey, ten years older, busied herself with the lunch box, cramming it into a microscopic space in the back seat of the overflowing Model T.

The only furniture from the log house saved for the wagon load which had left the day before was the almost-new icebox, a pump organ Albert had negotiated in a trade, two hump-backed trunks, a mahogany bed and a small twig table. Never partial to the twig furniture that had filled the log house in those early days after her arrival at the farm, Mabs had made a small concession in the case of the table. It would serve a purpose on the verandah of the new house.

Albert wanted to take one last walk through the log home before he left, but he knew Mabel would think he was demented. So, instead, he hied himself over to the drive shed and eased the car away from the building, pointing it toward the gate. The barnyards, as meticulously clean as always, had an eerie look about them. Not a bit of livestock in sight. The last heifer had been led out the day before by his longtime neighbour and friend, Alex Thom.

Mabs scrunched down on her haunches and scratched a match over the bottom of a chair, and touched it to the paper. She repeated the exercise until she had made her way entirely around the tower of furniture. The fire caught instantly, and Mabs backed away quickly to the cement pump platform and folded herself into a squatting position. She had waited a long time to see that blaze and she wasn't going to miss a minute of it! She could already see in her mind's eye the Arborite table she longed for with the steel edge running all around it, just like the one she saw every Saturday through the back door of Mrs. Stewart's kitchen in Renfrew when she was delivering eggs and butter and sticky buns. Grey, it was. That's what she'd get. Grey Arborite.

She heard Albert blow into his red dotted handkerchief. Well, let him snivel away. As far as Mabs was concerned, if she ever saw another piece of pine furniture as long as she lived it would be too soon for her! Hearing Albert did make her think of her boys, though, preparing to serve their country, although heaven knew where. She prayed silently, "Thank you, God, for allowing us this move. And may it be all we hope it will be. And take us safely to our new house. Well, God, it isn't new. But new to us. You know what I mean. Keep Emerson, Everett and Earl safe wherever they are."

The Model T was heaving gently just feet away from the pump. "Let's go, Mother," Mary said from a side window of the car. Audrey had squeezed into a space in the back seat much smaller than her frame, and she gave Mary a shove trying to gain another inch or two. Mabs picked up her purse from the ground and swiped off with her hand the coating of ashes that had drifted over. She paused to look back at the crackling fire. Transfixed for a moment, all thoughts of the present disappeared. She no longer heard the rumbling of the Model T or the impatient urgings of the girls. In each flame as it licked skyward, she saw her face and the faces of people past. She heard the sounds of the elevated trains as they thundered over the bustle and noise that was New York City. She slipped further back, to another place, another time…

Chapter One

May was unusually hot that year. Mabel tucked the sweater she had worn to school that morning through the strap of her bookbag and headed up the street that would take her past the Parliament buildings, past the old stone church and, finally, to Lyon Street and the tenement house she had lived in since she was born.

"Step on a crack and break your mother's back," she chanted, making sure her feet touched only solid pieces of sidewalk. In front of the church, the pavement narrowed and had been measured off into small squares to provide traction for the horses and buggies and cutters as they went up the slope into the churchyard.

Mabel stopped to deliberate. Should she step onto the road or should she walk over the cracks? The sun beat down on her black braids and left beads of perspiration on the end of her nose. She made her mind think of something else and walked over the span of small squares in the sidewalk.

She could hear laughter coming from Number 2 Firehall next door to the four-storey tenement. She had been warned against listening to the firemen who, her mother said, swore and told dirty stories. Mabel knew this was true because sometimes she pretended she was weeding the small garden against the board fence when she was really listening to the firemen, and even though she had no idea what some of the stories meant, she was sure they were dirty, because there were always roars of laughter and much thigh slapping when they talked.

That day, she could see the men through the cracks in the board fence. They were sitting on straight-backed chairs and fanning their faces with their black caps.

Mabel went through the little shed at the back of the downstairs apartment. She could smell the dank odour of stale water in the toilet, which was between the shed and the kitchen. The screen door slapped shut behind her and she tossed her sweater and book-bag on a kitchen chair. "Mama, I'm home."

She followed the faint sound of her mother's voice to the parlour. It was unusual to see Mama lying down at that time of day. She was almost always in the kitchen, peeling potatoes or setting the table. Today, Mama was on the couch. Not the one with the curved back, but the one with the iron springs that could be made into a bed. She had a cloth over her eyes, so Mabel thought she was tired and just resting. This was Monday, so that meant it was wash day. But Mama just motioned to Mabel and said only three words: "Get your father." When she pulled the cloth slowly from her face, Mabel was frightened by her mother's white pallor and sunken, dark-circled eyes. That wasn't the way Mama had looked this morning when Mabel was eating breakfast.

Mabel had been to Papa's workplace many times. But they had always taken a streetcar, because it went right into the streetcar tunnel under the bridge, where Papa made sure the cars ran properly and met the city's high standards. She had never gone on foot before. It was at least twenty blocks away, but Mabel bolted out the door and started running. Five blocks, ten blocks; she thought her chest would burst. "Get Papa, get Papa," she said over and over. Down the hill at Somerset Street, over the bridge and through the short tunnel. Her legs felt like rubber and her eyes stung from the sweat running off her forehead.

John Lapointe was standing with a paintbrush poised in the

direction of a brand new streetcar. His daughter had breath only to say, "Come…Mama's sick."

"Take the wagon," Joe said. Joe had worked with John Lapointe for almost twenty-five years. They played lacrosse together. The horse and wagon careened down the street under John's black leather whip, and when they rounded the corner at the firehall John was already jumping clear of the wheel. "Tend the horse," he hollered to no one in particular, and with Mabel close on his heels he ran in the street entrance of the house, knowing it would take more time to go down the cinder-covered yard and through the shed. Mary had complained of a "funny stomach" Sunday after mass, and again that morning. She was what his sister-in-law Vanetta called "delicate," and John protected her every way he could.

When Mabel got to the parlour, her father was on his knees beside the couch. Mama was very still. She wasn't talking to Papa, and the cloth that had covered her eyes had fallen onto the floor.

Mabel was wild-eyed with fear. Sure, Mama had been sick before, but she was always able to talk to her. Without looking away from his wife, John told Mabel to get her brothers. "I don't know where they are." Papa never stirred. "Find them. Go. I'll stay here with Mama."

Lou was where he shouldn't be—next door at the firehall. Amby was playing ball in the old hotel yard, two blocks away. Herby was sauntering home from school as if he had all day to get there. The youngest brother, Henry, had already seen Mama on the couch; when she wouldn't talk to him, he became terrified, ran to the woodshed, and hid behind a rain barrel filled with shovels and rakes and pieces of lumber.

The five children stood at the parlour door. Their father was in the same position he had been when Mabel ran from the house—

on his knees by the couch, holding Mama's hand. Saying nothing. But Mabel could see his jaw working as if he had a mouth full of food. Even though the house was hot and sticky, Papa reached up and pulled the plaid robe down from the back of the couch and gently covered Mama, even her face.

Mabel knew she was gone. Her mind raced back to the walk home from school, and the sidewalk in front of the church. "Step on a crack and break your mother's back."

<hr />

St. Joseph's Roman Catholic Church was cool. Mabel slid along the smooth seat and her four brothers, quieter than they had ever been in their lives, eased in beside her. She made her mind up to think of something other than the funeral service, which she didn't understand anyway because it was all in Latin. She tried not to look at the coffin. Aunts and uncles, everyone from the tenement house, and even the firemen from next door were there in their dress uniforms, helping to fill the cavernous church.

When they walked out of St. Joseph's into the blazing sun, which was bouncing off the sidewalk like hot coals, people shook Papa's hand, patted her brothers' heads, and crushed Mabel to their chests. The women smelled of lilac talcum powder, the men of hair tonic and perspiration.

The house on Lyon Street was quiet and dark when the Lapointes returned home. Every blind had been pulled down to keep out the sun. The gingerbread clock in the kitchen was striking twelve noon.

Without being told, Mabel and her brothers got out of their Sunday clothes. John called Mabel to the kitchen and told her she would have to make supper. "Can you manage that?" Mabel assured him she could. Her father had his valise beside him, and he was putting his dark pants in, along with his lacrosse shoes and the white shirt Mama had ironed last week.

"There is a tournament this afternoon." He seemed to be searching for the right words. "I am part of the team, you know. They are counting on me and I would be letting them down if I didn't play." There was a long pause. "You know, if I missed the game it still wouldn't bring Mama back."

She watched him from the parlour window as he crossed the road and climbed on the streetcar. Tears burned holes in her eyes and splashed on her blouse. She clenched and unclenched her fists as she watched the streetcar disappear with her father, who thought a lacrosse game was more important than mourning for the wife and mother no one would see again. Try as she might, Mabel could not understand what Papa had just done, and her chest heaved in anguish. Then her pain turned to anger.

There was no relief from the heat as the afternoon wore on. Mabel moved from room to room and went to the door in Mama and Papa's bedroom. Mama's clothes still hung at the back. Neat and on wooden hangers, just as Mama had left them. She put her face to the dress on top and pulled it into the crook of her neck.

Mabel peeled potatoes and took the leftover ham from the shelf in the cellar. She opened one of Mama's jars of beet pickles and sliced thick pieces of bread. The brothers ate the meal in silence, aware of the empty places at the table but saying nothing.

"Papa left me in charge. And we're not to go out of the house after supper. Lou and Herby, you help with reddin' up the kitchen, and Amby, you get Henry ready for bed." Mabel slipped into the role of guardian with ease, but already she had made up her mind this would be the last supper she would be making in the house on Lyon Street.

Chapter Two

Mabel had the smallest room in the flat. It had started out as a pantry. But Mama said that since Mabel was the only girl in a family of five, she should have a room of her own, and she had been sleeping there ever since young Henry was born. Mama had moved out the boxes and crates and clothes, put in a small cot and washstand, and hung a heavy drape in the doorless opening. The little room was off the kitchen, and since the family almost always used the back way in, she made sure her curtained door was pulled shut every night before she crawled into bed.

Since there was no other place for them, homemade preserves and pickles were still stored on two long wooden shelves along one wall. There was no window, but Mabel didn't mind—she was so happy to have a corner in the house that she could call her own. She had hung a picture of the Virgin Mary over her bed, and she thought it gave the room a look of serenity and peace.

That night, the brothers had taken a long time to settle down. Henry cried softly for Mama, but Mabel was able to soothe him with a cup of warm milk and a slice of bread. She looked at the clock on the shelf in the kitchen as she prepared for bed. It was just past ten. If Papa's team had won, he would be late getting home, because then they usually stopped at the hotel near the station for a beer. Mabel remembered the game was in Cornwall, so that meant he would be later than usual. All the better. She worked with quiet haste. First she took out a small valise from under her parents' bed. She folded in a sweater, her best shoes, some underwear and a dress that Mama had said she would quickly grow into if someone didn't soon put a brick on her head. Aunt Lily had given it to her, and Mabel loved its long pleated skirt and big white collar.

She took off her middy and skirt, folded them up and placed them under her bed. She put on the dress she had worn to Mama's funeral just hours before, and her long stockings, which were much too hot for May. But it would serve her purpose to look a little older than she was. She went into the parlor and looked at herself in the mirror over the velvet settee. The braids were a dead giveaway; only children wore braids. Oh well, she thought, I'll have to deal with them later.

Mabel sat at the kitchen table in front of a blank sheet of notepaper. She would have to be careful what she wrote, and think of how it would sound to Papa. Her head hurt, and she tried desperately to keep her thoughts clear, because somehow she had to convince Papa that what she was about to do was not done purely in anger. She had to let him know she loved him and her brothers, but that she had to do this or she would surely die, just like Mama. She began to write, in the big, childish, slanted letters that Sister Evangeline had spent the last four years trying to cure her of.

> *Dear Papa,*
> *When you get up in the morning, I will not be in my bed.*
> *Please do not worry as I will let you know where I am in*
> *a few days. Papa, you always said I was a big girl and*
> *could look after myself. I have taken my rosary with me*
> *and I know I will be safe. I ask you again not to worry.*
> > *I love you all,*
> > *Mabel*

She went to the tea can on the kitchen cupboard and propped the folded sheet of paper against it, knowing Papa would see it first thing in the morning. Then, fully dressed, she crawled under the light bed cover and concentrated on not falling asleep. The clock ticking in the kitchen sounded like thunder, and Mabel counted every strike. Papa was later than usual, but that was all right, because that meant he would go straight to bed when he got home.

Some time later, Mabel heard the back door open quietly. She could visualize every move her father was making: put down the valise. Empty pockets on the kitchen table. Go to the bathroom. Don't pull the chain. She knew he would tiptoe into her room and pause at the bed to make sure she was all right.

She could smell the faint odour of beer. He was going down the long, narrow hall to the bedroom at the front of the flat. She waited until the clock struck twice. She couldn't remember when she had last been awake at two o'clock in the morning. Last Christmas Eve maybe. She crawled out of bed, pushing back the heavy drape to let in the faint light shining through the kitchen window from the streetlamps outside. She pulled the covers up on the bed and straightened the pillow. Reaching under her bed, she quietly pulled out the valise. She groped along the kitchen table edge until her fingers closed around Papa's money purse. Taking it over to the window, Mabel was able to count out thirty-five dollars. Papa still had money left, enough to last him to Saturday, she hoped, when he got his pay from the Ottawa Electric Railway Company.

She tucked the money in the purse she had taken from Mama's dresser, adding it to the few dollars she had hoarded over the past years. Louis was always calling her a miser, saying she would "squeeze a penny till it hollered." Without looking back, Mabel quietly left the house by the back door and walked on the only grassy part of the yard, directly under the windows, one of which belonged to Papa's bedroom. She crouched down under the sill just in case he was still awake.

It took Mabel less than fifteen minutes to walk the eight long blocks to Union Station. Not a soul was on the Ottawa streets at that hour of the morning. The clock in the tower of the parliament buildings said it was fifteen minutes to three.

Her heels made a loud, hollow sound as they clicked on the marble floors of the station. She had been there many times before. Sometimes with Aunt Lily, who liked to watch the trains come in. And sometimes she and Papa would walk through the station when they had a bowl of soup at Bowles' Lunch.

She went to the only wicket she could see open and asked for a ticket to New York. The agent, who looked as if he couldn't wait to get off the night shift, yawned as he slammed his fist down on the punch and fed the ticket under the grate. Mabel counted out the money and was relieved to see that she had bills left over.

She walked along the outer wall of the waiting room so as not to attract attention. A porter was sleeping on one of the benches, and Mabel went up to him and gently touched his arm. He sprang awake as if he had been slapped. "Can you tell me which track the New York Central goes out on?" She added "sir" as an afterthought. The man unfolded himself from the seat and pointed down to the lonely waiting room. "Track three, miss." He didn't offer to carry the valise.

Mabel searched the numbers over the doors and read the destinations on the boards. Number three was the only gate open. She went through and walked to the first car she saw. A conductor was wiping the handles at the doorway. He took her valise and threw it up onto the top step. Then, with his hand under her elbow, he eased Mabel into the car.

She was panting, not from exertion, but from plain fear, and she fell into the first seat she came to. She was terrified to look out the window, so sure was she that she would see Papa's face searching for her. She held her small valise on her lap, and pushed her head back into the seat. She tucked Mama's purse between her hip and the inside arm of the seat. Taking three big silver hairpins out of her pocket, she wound her braids around her head, anchoring them tight. She had no idea how long it would take to reach New York. She thought she would probably have to go through Montreal. But she vowed she wouldn't leave that train until the conductor yelled out, "New York City."

Mabel was one month past her thirteenth birthday.

Chapter Three

Mabel had finally drifted off to sleep sometime after the conductor came down the aisle to collect the tickets. When she awakened she had a stiff neck and a big dent in her wrist where she had looped the handle of her valise. She had no idea what time it was, but her noisy stomach told her it must be long past noon hour.

She took out the paper bag of buttered bread and a piece of cheese she had brought from home and devoured it. Picking the crumbs off her skirt, she watched a woman get up and wobble down to the water cooler at the end of the car, bobbing from one seat to another. She was thirsty beyond belief, but vowed she wouldn't leave her seat until the train pulled into New York City. Her feet were "picky" from the long stockings, and one leg had gone to sleep, but Mabel sat bolt upright and tried to think of something else. Finally, she took her rosary out of the purse and said her beads. She said them again, cupping them in the palm of her hand. Suddenly she felt connected to Mama who had always said, "When you are frightened or don't know what to do, take out your rosary. It will always show you the way." Mabel saw the same woman who had gone for a drink open a small door and vanish inside. When she came out, she was rearranging her skirt. Perhaps it was the power of suggestion, but Mabel had to abandon the idea of staying in her seat until she reached her destination. She knew if she was going to make it to New York, she too would have to wobble down the aisle to what was obviously the bathroom.

The door slammed shut with a bang, almost knocking Mabel into the far wall. Over the toilet was a sign asking you not to flush while the train was standing in the station, which made perfect sense to her. The little sink was no bigger than a bread plate, but Mabel managed to wash her face and hands and dry them on her slip before opening the door and squeezing out into the aisle. A feeling of utter accomplishment swept over her. She was going to be just fine in New York City.

Had she been able to look ahead, or if her rosary could have given her any omen, Mabel might have stopped to ponder the wisdom of running off to a foreign city when she was barely into her teens. She probably would not have turned back (having inherited the Lapointe sense of adventure and the DeGray fortitude, two traits that would stand her in good stead for what lay ahead of her), but she might have gone into this new world, and new life, with more than a little apprehension. As it was, Mabel Ernestine Lapointe entered New York City at the age of thirteen full of hope and with an air of confidence usually worn by someone more worldly.

Chapter Four

The station was cavernous. Mabel thought it was the biggest place she had ever been in. It was sticky-hot and smelled as if the soot from the trains had permeated the very walls, or had followed the passengers in from the tracks outside. Mabel stood on the inside of the grilled sliding door to get her bearings. People shoved by her, many of them rushing to greet family or friends, and others, like Mabel, mesmerized by their surroundings and wondering what to do next.

Mabel put the cardboard valise down, trying to decide if she should walk towards one of the many doors leading outside, or if she should sit on one of the long benches until she could properly make up her mind. The decision was made for her when a woman wearing a fresh white tailored blouse, a rakish black-brimmed hat and a long, dark skirt came up and gently touched her on the arm. Mabel spun around.

"I'm with the Traveller's Aid. You look like you could use some help."

Without waiting to see if Mabel could or couldn't use some help, she propelled her over to a desk near a wall, and pointed to a straight-backed chair. "How old are you?"

"Eighteen."

The woman's eyebrows shot up into her hairline. Nonetheless, she wrote the information down on a long sheet of paper. "Name?"

"Mabel Ernestine Lapointe."

"Why are you in New York?"

Mabel almost said, "I'm an orphan," but she thought better of it. "I'm looking for a job. I came from Ottawa and I don't know a soul here. I need to find a place to stay."

The woman kept writing, and then she pulled a notebook out of her desk and leafed through it with fingers already showing signs of rheumatism, although she looked to Mabel as though she wouldn't be as old as Mama.

Minutes passed before the woman looked up from her book, and for the first time Mabel got a good look at her face. Mama would say she had kind eyes. Mama always said that about anyone who smiled easily. "I think we have just the place for you. The Traveller's Aid can pay for it for a week; if you haven't found a job by then, we can talk about helping you until you do."

"I have money. Almost twenty dollars." Mabel was about to dig into her purse to prove it when the woman told her to keep the money for an emergency, and repeated that she would look after the first week's rent. She took a key out of her pocket and fed it into the lock of the desk drawer, picked up her leather case, and before Mabel knew what was happening she was being herded out of the station onto the street.

"We can walk. Won't take us long. Are you too tired for that?" Mabel assured her she was fine, but she had a hard time keeping up with the woman as she darted in and out of the pedestrian traffic. Mabel would have liked to walk slower so that she could absorb her surroundings. She had never seen so many people. Even down in the market in Ottawa on a Saturday morning, there were never that many people. And everyone seemed to be in a hurry. There were no apologies when someone ran into her, and the gentlemen didn't bother to tip their hats as they did at home when they met a lady on the street.

Mabel's arms ached from carrying the suitcase and her purse, and she was too hot to put on the sweater she had carried all the way from Ottawa. Her feet hurt, and the long stockings were starting to twist around her legs; she felt as if the elastics holding them up were cutting her thighs in half. And still Miss Traveller's Aid charged on. The sun was slipping down behind the tallest buildings Mabel had ever seen. She tried to memorize the streets as they passed them, but they were all numbered. Fifty-second Street…or was it Fifty-fourth? She finally gave up.

When the woman finally slowed down, they were on a tree-lined street where the houses sat right on the sidewalk just like they did on Lyon Street at home. But the buildings looked newer and some had flower boxes on the window ledges, and they seemed to be attached to each other, not at all like the tenement house she had left, which stood alone on a corner.

The woman pulled a brass lever on a door leading into a brown brick house. She turned and smiled at Mabel. "You'll like it here. I hope Mrs. Munson has a room left. She is kept very busy by us, because we know the girls we bring here will be well looked after. She'll be just like your mother to you."

Mabel wanted to say, "No, she won't. Nobody will be like my mother. I wouldn't be here if my mother hadn't died on me." But she kept quiet about her sentiments and struggled with a smile.

The woman who answered the door was wrapped in a white pinny from her chin to her ankles. There were smudges of flour on her cheeks, and her grey, wiry hair was twisted in a knot on top of her head. Smells of something delicious floated out the door, and Mabel's stomach took a turn. She realized she was famished.

"This is Mabel. I hope you have a room for her, Mrs. Munson. She has just come from Ottawa to look for work. Of course, we will advance you the first week's rent. Hopefully, Mabel will soon find a job. Mabel is eighteen." The woman paused, putting great emphasis on Mabel's age. The two women looked at each other as if they shared some great secret, both with raised eyebrows and a slight wink, which didn't go unnoticed by Mabel.

"What a lucky day for you, Mabel. Violet—she was here almost four years—just moved out last week. Her room is at the front of the house. Would you like to see it before you make up your mind?"

Miss Traveller's Aid wasn't going to let Mabel make up her mind about anything. "I'm sure Mabel will like it just fine, Mrs. Munson. Now, here is my name and address, and someone from the Traveller's Aid is at the station every day and every night until midnight. If you need anything, anything at all, you mustn't hesitate to get in touch with us. That's what we're here for." She pushed a small note into Mabel's hand, and was gone, leaving the young girl and Mrs. Munson standing on the step.

Mabel followed her new landlady up a flight of stairs, and they circled a banister to the front of the house. Several doors were shut, but one at the end of the hall stood open. It wasn't a large room, but certainly a lot bigger than what Mabel was used to back home in Ottawa. And there was a window. Mabel had never had a window in her bedroom before. When she put her suitcase on the bed, Mrs. Munson immediately lifted it off and put it on a straight-backed chair. Mabel made a mental note not to do that again.

"You've missed supper. But give yourself a few minutes to settle and then come downstairs and I'll get a little plate ready for you." It was then Mabel realized her meals would be provided with the rent. That was good, because it meant she wouldn't have to buy food and cook it herself. If she was going to get a job it would be nice to come home to a good meal at night.

Mrs. Munson went out, closing the door behind her, and Mabel had a chance to look around the room. The bed was a lot bigger than the cot she slept on at home, and it was covered with a white, heavy spread with a raised pattern all over it. The dresser was big, too. With lots of drawers. And there was a little desk under the window with its own chair. A rocker was padded with bright green cushions that matched the curtains in the window. A footstool sat beside it. The room even had a clothes closet. There wasn't one room in the entire tenement house back home that had a real clothes closet. Mabel opened her suitcase and hung up the few things she had brought with her. She placed her underwear into one of the drawers. Mrs. Munson had laid out towels on the table beside the bed, and there was a brand new bar of soap sitting on top. Mabel knew there had to be a bathroom someplace, and she peeked out into the hall—towel, facecloth and soap in hand. She found what she was looking for when she spotted a white card tacked to a door.

> *Please do not hold up the bathroom. There are other people living here who use it as well. Your co-operation is appreciated.*
>
> Mrs. Elizabeth Munson

Although there didn't appear to be anyone else in the house (there wasn't a sound from any of the other rooms), Mabel washed her face quickly and hustled back to her room.

Her eyes swept the room again. Her first home away from her brothers and Papa—and, of course, Mama. A rush of homesickness swept over her, but she knew there wasn't one thing in the world she could do about that now. She headed downstairs, following the delicious smells emanating from somewhere behind the staircase.

Mrs. Munson had set a place at the kitchen table. The plate held cold chicken, tomatoes, sliced cucumbers and a large mound of potato salad. An orange, sliced and sprinkled with sugar, sat in a little fruit nappy. Buttered bread was on a side plate, and a small teapot sat beside a cup and saucer. Mabel noticed at once that all the dishes matched.

The landlady poured herself a cup of tea and sat down at the other end of the table. She settled into her chair like a hen nesting on a batch of eggs. Mabel, who was used to saying grace before she ate a meal, bowed her head and said her prayer silently. Mrs. Munson seemed to approve, because she said a soft "Amen" when Mabel raised her eyes.

Mabel hadn't eaten a meal for many hours, and she devoured the food as if it was to be her last meal on earth. Meanwhile, Mrs. Munson peppered her with questions about Ottawa and her family.

When every last morsel was gone, Mabel got up from the table and took her dishes to the sink, offering to wash up. Mrs. Munson didn't refuse the help, and the two of them chatted easily. The knot in Mabel's neck gradually eased, and the anxious ache in her stomach lessened.

It was starting to get dark outside when Mabel climbed the stairs and quietly headed to her room at the front of the house. "I'll just rest for a few minutes," she thought as she folded down the pristine white bedspread and stretched out on the quilt underneath. Within minutes she was asleep.

The New York night closed in around the brown brick house on Sixty-seventh Street, and the city's newest resident slept on, oblivious to the horses and carriages clacking by below. And unaware that someone in the house, three doors down from her own, would come into her life and change it forever.

Chapter Five

Mabel followed the smell of bacon and coffee to the room that ran the full length of the house across from the stairs. A long table was already set for breakfast and a clutch of young women sat around it, some talking and some intent on stuffing their breakfasts into their mouths. Mrs. Munson presided at the big buffet; when she spotted Mabel in the doorway, she came quickly and took her elbow, steering her to the one empty place at the table.

"This is Mabel. She will be living with us and is hoping to find work here in New York. I know you will make her welcome and help her any way you can. Please tell her your names. Sit there, Mabel, and help yourself."

With that Mrs. Munson swished by her to the kitchen, leaving Mabel looking into seven strange faces. It seemed like several minutes before anyone spoke, but it was really more like a few seconds, and then a girl with curly short hair and a more than ample figure, dressed in a navy blue skirt and blouse that looked like a uniform, reached her hand across the table.

"I'm Rosie. You must be in Violet's room at the front. I'm just down the hall from you. Been here at Mrs. Munson's for three years. You'll like it once you get used to all the rules."

There was a round of snickers at the table. "Ya, like spending only five minutes in the bathroom," someone offered. "And putting your lights out at ten o'clock," added a girl with more freckles than Mabel had ever seen in her life.

Rosie washed down the last corner of toast with a swig of coffee and asked Mabel what kind of work she was interested in.

"I'll work at anything. I really don't care, as long as I get a job."

Rosie seemed to ponder the information and looked as if she was filing it somewhere important in her mind. "I'm going to work now, and if you want me to, I'll come and get you on my lunch hour and show you the store where I've been since I came to New York. It's just a short walk, and you never know, you might find a job there. I know they hired a new girl in the shoe department last week. Do you know anything about selling?"

Mabel hated to admit she knew precious little about work of any kind, unless you could call minding her brothers and peeling potatoes work. "I've never worked in a store, but I would be willing to learn." She was pleased that she had been clever enough to sidestep the fact that she had never really held a job of any description.

"That's all it takes at Macy's…being willing to learn and owning a strong back." There were chuckles again around the table.

Rosie took Mabel's silence for an acceptance and said she would be back shortly after twelve o'clock. One by one the girls rose from the table, picking up their dishes as they did and toting them out to the kitchen. Mabel followed suit, watching everyone move. The sooner she fitted into the routine, the better she would get along at Mrs. Munson's.

The house suddenly became as quiet as it had been the previous night when Mabel had arrived. She went back up to her bedroom and wondered how she would fill in the time between then and the noon hour. She looked out the window; the street below had come alive with people and vehicles and horses and carts all rushing in opposite directions. Mabel marvelled that no one got run over. The air was heavy and a mist hung over the tall buildings like a gossamer shawl. The building directly across the street looked like a warehouse and a big sign was propped on the roof advertising a hair tonic for men. Papa used hair tonic. He had to or his hair would stand straight up on end. Mabel could almost smell the sweet odour of hair tonic in that room in New York and she finally succumbed to the homesickness that swept over her like a heavy blanket. She buried her face in the pillow of her bed and it was soon wet from her tears. She wondered if she had enough money to go home.

Then she thought of that last day, the day Mama was buried,

and how Papa had gone off to his lacrosse game. And Mama not cold in the ground. How could Papa do that? How could he think of lacrosse even if it was a tournament game, when he had just buried his wife and the mother of his children? The anger was still there, which was a good thing. Mabel shook herself from her feelings of self-pity and washed her face, combed her hair, wrapped her braids around her head…and waited for her new friend Rosie.

<hr/>

Macy's Department Store was huge, certainly much bigger than any store Mabel had ever seen in Ottawa. Rosie said she ran the elevator there, and only that morning she had been told that she was being moved in two weeks to the shipping department which, she had been told, was one step up from running an elevator. She rolled her eyes as if she didn't believe the story for a minute. "I thought maybe you could try for the job, Mabel."

"I have never even been on an elevator. I wouldn't know what to do. Someone told me they are pretty dangerous, and my friend Beth said she knew someone who fell down the place where the elevator goes up and down and she was crushed to death."

Rosie threw her head back and laughed, showing teeth that looked as though they might have been taken off a piano keyboard. "Well, I've been running an elevator for two years and I have never had five seconds' trouble. I'll tell you what. When we get to the store, you go one way and I'll go another. We'll pretend we don't know each other. Head for the elevator…you can't miss it, there's a big sign with an arrow pointing right at it. Get on, and I'll show you there is nothing to be afraid of, and if there are no customers on it, I'll even give you a few lessons."

With that Rosie charged into Macy's, leaving Mabel with no

choice but to follow and look for the elevator sign.

It hung on a chain in the middle of an aisle. With extreme caution, Mabel headed in the direction of the red arrow. Two big brass doors were closed and Mabel joined a woman who had parcels in her arms and looked as if she was well acquainted with Macy's Department Store.

Noiselessly, one of the brass doors slid open and there was Rosie standing just inside the door. She had added white wrist-length gloves to her uniform. The woman customer moved to the back of the elevator, and Mabel did likewise. Rosie pushed a big brass lever on the wall just inside the door in an arc and, much to Mabel's concern, the elevator started to move. She wanted to hang on to something, but there was nothing inside but the highly polished wood walls. The elevator cruised to a stop and Rosie, in a sweet and gentle voice, said, "Second floor." The woman at the back headed out the door, leaving Rosie and Mabel alone.

"Now, come over here and I'll show you how it's done." Mabel worked her way around the elevator as if she were walking the edge of a flat-topped roof. "All you do is shove that handle down to the next floor and the elevator does the rest. On the way down, you just push the lever the other way." She opened her hands, palms up. "Simple. That's all there is to it. Here, try it."

The last thing Mabel wanted to do was to be responsible for her new friend's early demise, or for her own, for that matter. Rosie had to guide Mabel's hand to the lever and hold it there. To Mabel's utter amazement the elevator moved as gently as a breeze. They repeated the performance until the elevator had gone to the top floor, Rosie being sure not to open the doors so that no one, especially a store manager, would see what she was up to.

By the time the two girls had gone up and down Macy's Department Store from top to bottom at least five times, Mabel had the hang of it. "Now, I'm going to let you off on the third floor. Go to the very back of the store and ask for the office manager. He is the one who does the hiring. And tell him you have had experience in running an elevator. Don't let on you know anyone here. They're fussy about making sure the employees are neither related to anyone who works here, or know any of the staff personally. And Mabel, for goodness sake, stop shaking."

Twenty minutes later, Mabel was handed a navy skirt and blouse and two pairs of new, white cotton gloves and told to report to work the next morning. No one had asked her how old she was.

A young Lapointe family in Ottawa: from left, Henry, John, Amby, Mabel, Herby and Lou (standing)

Henry (left) and Amby
visiting with Mabs
in New York

Herby (seated) with
Henry (left) and Amby

John Lapointe with sons
Louis (left) and Herby

Amby Lapointe
circa 1920

Chapter Six

Two years had passed since Mabel had first set foot in New York City. She had bobbed her hair and wore it parted in the middle. It was thick enough to fit right in with the hairstyle of the day, when every woman of consequence had her hair cut short as a sort of emancipation pronouncement (although Mabel's emancipation had taken place the moment she climbed on board the New York Central out of Ottawa). She had grown in height, put weight on where it mattered, and looked far older than her years. The original girls at Mrs. Munson's rooming house had gone on to other environs, leaving only Rosie and Mabel. Others had taken their places, of course, but Rosie was the one who had taken Mabel under her wing. Rosie and Mabel had become fast friends.

"I hate Mabel for a name," Rosie blurted out soon after the two had met. Rather than being offended, Mabel assured Rosie she wasn't any more fond of the name than she was, and that she much preferred "Mabs". And so it was that everyone, even Mrs. Munson, called the young French Canadian Mabs. Although letters from Papa still came addressed to Miss Mabel Ernestine Lapointe.

Mabs was now writing to Papa weekly. He wrote terse notes in reply, not telling her much about her four brothers, but rather admonishing her for leaving home and causing him worry beyond measure. Long after Mabs had assured him that she was well, had a good job, was paying her own way, and had no intention of going back to Ottawa, Papa Lapointe still barbed his notes with reprimands and censure.

But Mabs had moved beyond concern for what Papa thought. She was a woman now. She got lonesome sometimes, but the very thought of leaving New York and Rosie and her job running elevators at Macy's Department Store always jolted her back to reality. She could no more go back home than she could fly across the ocean. Either prospect was beyond her comprehension. And so she settled into life in New York, going to shows when she could afford them, walking in Central Park on Sunday afternoons, often with Rosie and a few new friends she had made at work. She got paid every two weeks. In cash. She handed over eight dollars to Mrs. Munson for her room and board, bought some new clothes and kept any remaining money under her mattress in a big brown envelope. She still didn't trust banks.

"Do you see yourself doing this five years from now?" Rosie asked one day when they were sitting on a park bench throwing crusts of bread to the pigeons.

"What do you mean? Sitting here feeding pigeons?"

"No, of course not. I mean working at Macy's."

Mabs pulled her eyes from the flock of pigeons around their feet and, catching a glimpse of clear New York sky overhead, without giving the question more than a few seconds' thought, answered, "I want to be a nurse. Someday. I have an aunt who is a nurse back home. She is the kindest person I know. Married a doctor, too. I don't care about marrying a doctor, but I would most certainly like to be a nurse. That's what I'm saving my money for. As soon as I have enough I'll quit Macy's and go into training. Rosie, do you think they would take me when I'm only fifteen or sixteen years old?"

Rosie pushed a crust of bread away from her with a toe of her shoe, towards a pigeon that was bolder than the rest. Rosie had long since guessed that Mabs wasn't as old as she let on.

"I doubt it. I think you have to be at least eighteen. But look how fast the past two years have gone by. You'll be eighteen before you know it. You know, I have always wanted to be a nurse too. But of course it wasn't possible for me. Mama said it would be easier for a Jewish girl to slip through a keyhole than it would be for her to become a nurse."

It was the first time Mabs realized Rosie was Jewish.

Rosie Vineberg was the youngest in a family of four. Her two older sisters, Ethel and Bernice, were married and her brother, who was next to her, was suitably matched with a nice Jewish girl who had Mrs. Vineberg's approval. Ethel's husband, according to Rosie, was only half Jewish; Bernice's husband nobody talked about. Rosie thought he was Russian or something like that. "Mama gave up on Bernice when she started keeping company with an Irish Catholic. She said she would never amount to a hill of beans. And then when she married Ivan it was like she had died. I like Ivan. Even if he does pinch me where he shouldn't. But he does it right in front of Bernice, so I guess there isn't much harm in it."

Rosie felt it was her duty to look after Mabs. She knew nothing about living in a city like New York, and Rosie had learned early in the game that a young girl could be "chewed up and spit out" if she didn't know how to take care of herself. So when Mrs. Munson took in a male roomer, "only for a few weeks" she had said, Rosie told Mabs she would have to keep her eyes open and her knees together. There were no locks on the bedroom doors, so Rosie showed Mabs how to tuck the back of her chair under the doorknob before she went to bed at night.

"Sleep with your bloomers and your vest on. And anchor the two of them together with pins. I have heard there are some men who carry chloroform in a bottle and before you know it they can put you to sleep and do whatever they want with you, and you wouldn't even know they were in the room. I don't like the look of that fellow. Did you see the way his eyes come together? And that greased hair reminds me of someone I saw in a circus once. So you be careful, Mabs. You're young and pretty. Just his type. He'd never bother with me, but I won't take any chances either. I'll sleep with my bloomers pinned to my vest too."

Mabs went to bed that first night the new boarder came to stay with a chair rammed under the doorknob and her bloomers and vest pinned together, as instructed. The first thing she did in the morning was check to see if the pins were still in her underwear.

After three weeks Mabs was reasonably sure Rosie had been mistaken about the man with the oiled hair. He hardly spoke a word at mealtimes, and no one even found out where he worked. But Mabs still wasn't taking any chance. "Still waters run deep," Rosie had said. Whatever that meant.

One morning, as Rosie and Mabs came down the stairs together, the man was standing beside his suitcases in the front hall. He was shuffling from one foot to the other, and it was obvious he was waiting to say his goodbyes to the two girls whose only approach to him had been at the table in Mrs. Munson's dining room.

He handed Mabs and Rosie a small card and said if they ever needed his services to get in touch with him. And then he opened the door and went out into the cold New York morning. Mabs waited until she was seated in front of her porridge and then she took the card out of her skirt pocket. Dr. Raine De Silva, Hackensack New Jersey Hospital, she read. She flipped the card over. "I heard you talking to your friend about being a nurse. If I can help, please write me."

Mabs was so excited she couldn't eat her porridge, but Rosie took care of it, as well as the half-eaten pieces of toast on Mabs' butter plate. Rosie didn't believe for one minute that he was a doctor. "He's too oily to be a doctor. And too young too. I'm going to ask Mrs. Munson." And she let out a war whoop that could probably be heard in the next block. "Mrs. Munson, was that guy a doctor? What was he doing in New York if he works at a hospital in New Jersey?"

Mrs. Munson came out of the kitchen wiping one hand on her big white apron and shaking a spoon in Rosie's general direction with the other. "Young lady, I don't appreciate being yelled at like that. Now, what's all this about?"

A quieter Rosie re-asked her questions.

"Yes, he's a doctor. And he was here in New York getting extra training. Something to do with bones or rheumatism, I think. I can't imagine why you would care, you never gave the poor man the time of day when he was here." And she banged her way back to the kitchen, slamming the door behind her.

Mabs took the stairs three at a time to put Dr. De Silva's card in a place of safekeeping…right under her mattress with her money. She'd write to him that very night. Just maybe Dr. De Silva could help her get accepted in the nurses' training course in New Jersey.

"Oily. That's what he is, oily," Rosie said when Mabs and she were having their lunch at the store. "Can you imagine having him operate on you? Boy, you'd sure want to be sure there were plenty of safety pins holding your underthings together."

Chapter Seven

Mabs wrote to Dr. De Silva that very night. She had bought a box of fine white stationery at Macy's. The paper she used to write to

Papa was coarse and lined; it would never do. This new writing paper had watermarks in it, and Miss Staples in stationery said it was just about the best you could buy.

When she was finished she went down the hall and rapped on Rosie's door. Rosie would know if the letter was worded properly and if she didn't sound too forward. Rosie was sitting cross-legged on her bed, which was quite a feat for Rosie, since her legs were short and stocky. She was knitting mittens for Ethel's daughter. Bright red wool to match a scarf she had already finished. She read Mabs' letter and let out a big sigh, which caused the bed to heave and which Mabs immediately took as a sign that Rosie wasn't too impressed.

"You sure you want to do this? Shouldn't you at least tell him how old you are? Wait until he learns you are a few months short of your sixteenth birthday. You know, Mabs, before you go much further with this, you're most certainly going to have to tell somebody how old you are. I have no idea how you have been able to keep it from personnel at Macy's for this long."

"Because I do a good job. Have you ever heard one complaint about me? Has anyone ever said I don't work hard? I polish those brass levers and that door grill on the elevator at least twice a day; my gloves are always spotless. Who cares how old I am as long as I can do the job?" Mabs could feel frustration creeping into her body like a chill.

Rosie dismounted from the bed and put the letter back in Mabs' hand. She stood with a fist on her hip and her chunky feet planted firmly on the braided mat at the side of the bed. "Why don't we deliver the letter? That would be better than mailing it. Mama has been telling me it's time I went home for a visit, and we could both go to Hackensack after work on Saturday, go over to the hospital and hand the letter to Dr. De Silva in person."

As if Mabs had already agreed to the plan, Rosie continued. "We'll go on the train as soon as we finish and come back Sunday night. Of course, we'll have to clear it with old eagle-eyes Munson first."

And so it was decided. Mrs. Munson read off a litany of do's and don'ts, and behind her Rosie rolled her eyes and wagged her head, mouthing her words silently. Mabs glued her eyes to Mrs. Munson, knowing full well that if she looked at Rosie, even for a second, she would collapse in hysterics.

It was raining softly when Mabs and Rosie exited by the employee door at the back of the building. They shared an umbrella and huddled together as they ran for the train depot. It was the first time Mabs had left New York City since she had come from Ottawa, and once again she was amazed at the immensity of everything around her. It seemed to her that thousands of people were teeming onto the train, newspapers folded under their arms, briefcases and leather bags swinging from their hands, and everyone fighting for a seat. It took Rosie, aggressive and pushy, pulling Mabs by the hand, to find a side bench in the very last car. By the time the train had left the city, the sun had sunk low in the sky.

The Vineberg house was a copy of a dozen others on a tree-lined street. A walkway led to a small verandah and Mabs noticed a woman's face looking out from behind a lace curtain. She quickly dropped it when she saw the two girls, and by the time they reached the house, the door had been swung open and someone who looked like an older version of Rosie met them on the top step.

"It's about time you come to see your old mother. And look at that skirt, would you? It couldn't be much shorter and still be decent. Come in, come in, for goodness' sake. The neighbours will think you aren't welcome in your own home." The words were acute, but the tone was soft and enveloping. She pulled Rosie to her and stroked the back of her head and then stood back and looked at her as if she hadn't seen her for many years.

Rosie presented Mabs, who had hung back at the door, and pointed out to her mother that her skirt was not considered short by the day's standards. Her ankles were just barely showing, and many of the girls Rosie worked with wore their skirts much shorter than that. Some of them almost to the calves of their legs.

Floating aromas of garlic and savoury chicken met them head-on in the front hall. Mrs. Vineberg instructed Rosie to take Mabs upstairs with her suitcase and make her comfortable in the front room, and then to come down, because they would soon be sitting down for the evening meal.

Later, when the two girls had washed the dishes and stacked them on the open shelves in the spotlessly clean kitchen, they headed up the stairs to retrieve Mabs' letter, which had been placed between sheets of newspapers to keep it from wrinkling. "Hackensack Hospital is not more than three blocks from here," Rosie said. "I think we should go first thing in the morning and see if we can find Dr. De Silva. He may not be working on a Sunday, but if he isn't there we can leave the letter with someone."

The walk over to the hospital took no more than fifteen minutes. Rosie had run a comb through her unruly hair and tucked a new tube of lip rouge in her pocket to be put on when they were well away from the house. The morning air was cool and refreshing, made more so by the gentle rain of the previous day.

Closer to the hospital the houses were very different from the Vinebergs'. They were long and narrow with shallow walkways between them. Rosie said they were called railroad flats because they looked like boxcars. "We used to live in one a few years ago. Just before I moved to New York. But Mama hated it, and when Papa got a job at the Acme Dress Factory, they rented the house they are in now. Mama said if things work out at the factory they'll probably buy the house. Papa is really a pattern maker, but right now he's in the packing room. But Mr. Hessler, he owns the factory, said as soon as there is an opening he will move Papa into patterns."

The two girls walked along, coming to a small park area at the end of the first street. Rosie dropped herself onto a bench and scrounged in her pocket for her lip rouge. "If you think Mama was upset over the length of my skirt, you should see her when one of her daughters puts on lip rouge. Beatrice was married before she was allowed to wear it."

Mabs sat entranced, watching Rosie jab at her mouth with the lip rouge, making a perfect outline of her lips without the benefit of a mirror. Obviously Rosie had done this before. The transformation was immediate. Rosie's face glowed with the added colour, and for the first time Mabs took notice of her radiant olive complexion, and her dark, bobbed hair perfectly framing her face. She had worn a middy blouse, white with long navy ties under the collar, and a straight navy skirt barely touching the tops of her shoes. She looked like one of the young ladies who shopped in the dress salon at Macy's, rather than someone who had once run the store elevator and now wrapped parcels for delivery. It gave Mabs great satisfaction that her friend Rosie was a young woman of distinction.

Rosie knew how to make the most of her appearance. She was naturally full-bodied. Barely five feet tall, she looked heavier than she really was. But the white blouse and slim navy skirt took pounds off her, and Mabs—as she had done so often over the past two and a half years of their friendship—admired Rosie's flawless complexion, beautiful dark eyes, and a face that always had a look of anticipation. When Mabs thought about it, as she did on that walk to the Hackensack Hospital, she appreciated that her friend Rosie was a "real looker", as Stan in the men's wear department had said many times. Rosie wasn't interested in Stan, though.

The Hackensack Hospital looked like an enormous estate house. Its clapboard exterior was painted stark white; the buildings had pillars in the front and shutters on each window, making it look more like a Victorian mansion than a hospital. It had had several additions since being taken over by the board of governors in 1888, but inside, its sole purpose was clearly "to care for the sick and mend the broken."

Rosie went right up to the desk just off the entrance and boldly asked for Dr. Raine De Silva. The young woman, not much older than Rosie herself, said it would take several minutes to find Dr. De Silva, and that even then he might not be available. "I saw him earlier. But most likely he is making the rounds and can't be disturbed. Could I say who is asking for him, and perhaps give him a message?"

Rosie pulled herself up to her full height, which was considerably shorter than the young woman standing at her station. "We are prepared to wait for him. You may tell him that Rosie Vineberg and Mabs Lapointe are here to see him. But if he is too busy now, we will just sit in the vestibule until he is free."

The receptionist emitted a deep sigh, and with a look of resignation headed off down the hall, her rubber-heeled shoes making not a sound on the wooden floor. Rosie and Mabs moved over to the polished bench just inside the door.

Occasionally a nurse in white, starched uniform and crisp cap rustled by, but no one stopped to ask them their business. The two prepared for a long wait. They knew little about doctors and less about hospitals, but they were reasonably sure Dr. De Silva wouldn't be making an appearance for a goodly while.

Mabs was enthralled with the Hackensack hospital. She took in every last detail of the few nurses she saw. Starched, bibbed aprons. Some with striped uniforms underneath, all with a small pair of scissors tucked in the back waistbands. The nurses' only sounds came from the crisp starch of their uniforms as they floated almost noiselessly down the long corridors.

A door with frosted panels opened and Mabs caught her breath as she saw Dr. Raine De Silva. He came right over to the bench, took Mabs' outstretched hand and then bowed low to Rosie. He wore a long white coat over his suit. Mabs was sure she could trust him with her life.

"I didn't expect to see either of you so soon. I'm glad you took me up on my invitation to get in touch with me. I suppose, Mabs, you are here to ask about your chances of getting into nursing?"

It was Rosie who answered. "I think there is something you should know. You see, Mabs is not yet sixteen. She has written you a letter. Perhaps you should read it and then we could talk." Rosie elbowed Mabs, and Mabs took the letter from her purse, being especially careful not to bend it.

"Let's go outside on the verandah. I can take a few minutes now." Dr. De Silva took Rosie's elbow, and Mabs was left to fend for herself. Raine De Silva took the letter out of its envelope and scanned its contents quickly.

"Well, certainly your age will be a problem. They may take you after you turn seventeen, but I am very sure they would consider that fifteen is much too young to take on the responsibilities that go with nurses' training. I would suggest you stay at your job for at least another year, and then I can see what we can do. I expect I will still be at this hospital; I hope to specialize in orthopedics, and they do a lot of that work here."

Rosie hung onto every word Dr. De Silva said, and for an entirely different reason than did Mabs. Clearly Rosie now regarded Dr. De Silva with respect. Gone were her first impressions made in haste back at Mrs. Munson's boarding house.

Dr. De Silva took his watch out of his pocket and pressed the stem, which opened the lid to reveal the time. "I have to go back. I am in surgery in an hour and I want to go over my patient's charts. But I will keep in touch." He looked directly at Rosie, who was beaming and fidgeting with her gloves and smiling up into his face.

On the way back to New York, Rosie was pensive. Mabs felt something special had happened to Rosie between the time they had arrived at the Hackensack Hospital and the time they waved goodbye to Dr. De Silva. Little did she know that a great deal had happened. Yes, a great deal indeed. Rosie had fallen in love.

Chapter Eight

Hackensack Hospital
Second Street,
Hackensack, New Jersey

Dear Papa,

Your much appreciated letter arrived yesterday, and I was so pleased to hear that you are well and that your lacrosse team is having such a good season. I am well, and enjoying my training here very much. Matron said she thinks I will make a fine nurse. The work is hard and the hours long, but I received my cap in a special ceremony and I was proud and determined to work even harder during my final years here.

I have spoken to you before about my good friend Rosie Vineberg. Well, I have what I think is wonderful news. She is going to be married to Dr. Raine De Silva! He is the doctor who was paramount in getting me accepted here as a nurse-in-training in spite of my being several months shy of my eighteenth birthday at the time.

It is a sad time here in New York as so many of the young men are going off to war. Raine may have to go too, but at the present time his is considered an essential service to his country. He is very well known and respected in his field and his shoes would be hard to fill if he were sent to the war.

It is a worry for you too, I know, now that Louis and Herby have joined the army. I am grateful that Amby and Henry are too young to don the uniform, although perhaps by the time they have come of age, they too will have to join the forces. Let us pray this terrible war will be over by then.

There is little time for a social life here. Raine and Rosie try to keep me involved in their lives, and this weekend, when I shall enjoy my very first two days off since I came here, I shall meet them in New York. Raine has many friends in New York, as that is where he was born and where his parents still live.

Please do not worry about me, Papa. I am very happy doing what I have always wanted to do. I know you would want and expect me to do my job well, and I shall work hard so that I won't disappoint you, or myself.

I will write again very soon, and send you a picture of myself in my new cap. Matron had our pictures taken and she had copies made for all of us. There are eleven in my nursing class, and we have all become good friends.

I send my abiding love to you and my brothers and I continue to say my rosary every day just as Mama would want me to do, and I pray for safe keeping for all of you.

Mabel Ernestine Lapointe
June, 1917

Chapter Nine

"I don't have to tell you, Mama would be much happier if Raine was a Jew. She likes him well enough, although I guess that has more to do with his being a doctor than with anything else."

Rosie and Mabs were waiting for Raine to appear. He had come to New York from Hackensack on the same train as Mabs, but had to meet a friend before lunch. It was a hot Saturday in mid-August, and Mabs was happy to be out of her nurse's uniform for a few hours. Although she loved the stark white of the starched bibs and cap, getting into a simple dress was a relief. Rosie, as usual, since she and Raine had announced their wedding plans, was radiant and chatted on about Mabs being her maid of honour, how Raine and his best friend were at that very minute signing a deed for a double house near Gramercy Park. They would live in one half, and lease the other side. Raine would join the multitude of commuters going and coming daily between New York and New Jersey. Mabs was delighted for Rosie.

Rosie said Raine's father had helped his doctor son finance the purchase of the house. "And our friend Mario (you'll like Mario, Mabs) got money from *his* father, and so they were able to buy the house together without any hardship. Gramercy Park is a lovely area, with wonderful, prestigious houses, and we're right around the corner from Lexington Avenue, and there is a huge church there. And guess what—our house isn't too far from where David Graham Phillips, the famous author, was murdered." Rosie lowered her voice and her eyes, as if she was relating a horror story of great magnitude, which indeed she was. But Mabs had no idea who David Graham Phillips was, and she certainly wasn't interested in seeing the site of a murder!

It was while both young ladies were in this state of silent reflection that Raine and his friend appeared. They approached the park bench, Raine animated and slapping his friend on the back as if they were sharing some wonderfully funny joke. The man with Raine was tall and had hair as black as ink, and as they got closer Mabs was struck by the contrast between the coal-black hair and the dark red mustache shadowing his top lip. Mabs wondered if he had perhaps had the mustache dyed. Rosie, of course, had met Mario many times, as they had shared some happy evenings together as a trio.

Mario Saijai was tall. Raine was tall too, but Mario was a good hand taller. His skin was dark and his eyes were brown and fringed in the longest lashes Mabs had ever seen on a man. He was quite handsome, she thought, as he bent low over her hand and brushed his lips across her white glove.

"Let's go to the Automat," Mario said. "It's the best bargain in town. Then we can go off to the zoo. It's a great day for walking. You'll like the zoo today, Mabs. I haven't been there for two or three years, and since then they have acquired a sloth bear from India. I want to sketch it for my portfolio."

Mario talked in short, fast sentences, leaving little time or opportunity for the others to interject or add their voices or opinions. But rather than seeing his suggestions as an irritant, Raine, Rosie and Mabs accepted them and the four of them started off for the Automat. Mabs and Rosie ate there often; still, Mabs never ceased to be amazed at how you could put a nickel in the slot, open the glass door, and your lunch would be there on a plate.

After they had claimed their food, they sat at one of the square wooden tables, and the chatter swirled around Mabs' head. She was barely able to take in everything that was said. Raine put his hand over Rosie's. "Well, it's all signed, sealed and delivered. We own the house. And as soon as we get back from our honeymoon we can move right in."

Mario ate his lunch with fervour, adding, between bites, that since he owned one half of the house, it seemed logical that he should get married too. In that way they wouldn't have to go looking for a suitable tenant. Everyone chuckled, including Mabs, who could feel her cheeks turn scarlet. She guessed Mario was at least twenty-four years old, and here she was barely eighteen. But she certainly wouldn't mind sharing a house with Mario Saijai.

The New York Zoological Park was the centre of what Mabs knew to be Bronx County. Although the zoo was miles away, the four young people walked and laughed and talked about everything from nursing to bone surgery to the responsibility of being land owners. When they came to a street corner, Mario would take Mabs' hand and place it in the crook of his arm. She thought she had never been as happy in New York as at this very moment in time.

It was late afternoon when they reached the zoo, and they paused at the gate to read the brass sign: "The New York Zoological Zoo is maintained by the Zoological Society, and is here for the pleasure of those who share the love of animals and who are concerned about their preservation." Mario and Raine knew exactly where they were going. The cage was big and the sloth bear, stretched out on its back, had exaggerated long black hair and a white muzzle. Its claws too were long and pure white. Mario commented that it was this bear that Kipling called "Baloo". Mabs made a mental note to get Kipling's books from the Hackensack Library, which she had joined shortly after entering nursing.

Mario and Raine were very knowledgeable on many subjects, but Mabs was not the least surprised that Rosie had no trouble keeping up with them. Rosie had taken it upon herself to improve her mind. After all, Raine had been to university, and if she was going to be a doctor's wife she had better start educating herself. A higher education was not high on the Vinebergs' list of priorities, although hard work and a sense of responsibility were. By the time Raine had proposed marriage, Rosie had been promoted several times at Macy's and was now in charge of all the staff on the third floor.

Mario found a bench near the bear's cage and he motioned for the others to sit. He sat with crossed legs on the grass and opened a large envelope he had been carrying. He removed a flat pad and several pencils. Mabs was about to ask what he was going to do when Raine put his finger to his lips to gently silence her. It was obvious Raine was used to this routine of Mario's. Mabs was close enough to see over his shoulder and she watched as Mario, with quick, sure strokes, pencilled the bear, adding shrubs and stumps where none existed.

The sun was low when he finished. Without showing it to anyone, he brought the cover sheet over the pad and tucked it back into the envelope. "We'll take a taxi back to the city," he said. Mabs was grateful for his take-charge attitude. She was sure she couldn't walk another step.

Rosie still maintained a room at Mrs. Munson's rooming house.

It was getting dark when they approached the house, and the lights were on. Everything looked warm and inviting. Mrs. Munson was delighted with Rosie's impending marriage, and she welcomed the young people into the house that night and offered them a light supper. Rosie, ever mindful of saving her money for her marriage, wondered if Mrs. Munson would tack the cost of "four light suppers" to her twice monthly room and board. Her mind was put at ease when Mrs. Munson said in the kitchen, "It is wonderful to have young people around. Especially in the evenings, which can get so long when all you ladies go off to your rooms. And, of course, I wouldn't think of charging you for this light supper, Rosie. But if I may, I would like to ask your Dr. De Silva about my knees; they're giving me so much trouble lately."

And so it transpired that often the four young people would meet at Mrs. Munson's rooming house, go off to enjoy one of the many places of entertainment, and return later in the evening for a light repast, which usually meant freshly baked bread, a cheese plate, cold meatloaf and hard-boiled eggs. Naturally, Mrs. Munson always managed to ask Raine some important medical question, which he patiently answered in detail.

Mabs' days off were few and far between, and sometimes if she only had a few hours to call her own, Raine, Mabs and Mario would wait for her at the nurses' residence called The Hall. Afterwards, in one of the little cafes for which Hackensack was becoming famous, they would sit and talk and drink coffee.

In this way, as Raine and Rosie's marriage date drew closer, Mario and Mabs developed a relationship akin to a quiet romance. There was never any overt show of affection. It was just understood that they were "a couple", a situation that seemed to please Mario and that brought Mabs the greatest joy and contentment of her short lifetime.

Mabs couldn't imagine life being more complete. She was a year off being a full-fledged nurse, she had a dear friend in Rosie whom she loved as a sister, and Mario was showing much more than a passing interest in her. Life was good.

Chapter Ten

When Mabs was lucky enough to get "an overnighter", she spent the time in New York. Mrs. Munson let her use a small cot in the back room which was kept for storing linens for the house. She always refused the dollar Mabs would offer.

Mrs. Munson was thrilled to be so involved in the upcoming marriage of one of her tenants—especially Rosie Vineberg's wedding, since she had been at the rooming house for so many years.

"Came as a wee bit of a thing, with nothing more than a few scraps of clothes and enough money for her first week's lodging. Now look at her. She has a very important position…"—Mrs. Munson ceased calling it a mere job when Rosie became engaged to Dr. De Silva—"she is going to be living in a home near Gramercy Park, and I am invited to the wedding," Mrs. Munson was happy to pass on this information to anyone on the street who would listen.

Elizabeth Munson had indeed become very fond of the four young people. Dr. De Silva, tall, with sharp features and what Mrs. Munson called the "kindest eyes I have ever seen on a man," treated the rooming house like his second home. Mario Saijai, as well, felt at ease in the big, rambling building that had been home to countless young girls over the years.

Raine was shy and rarely showed emotion. Mario, on the other hand, was almost boisterous. He would grab Mrs. Munson and waltz her around the parlour, or he would grab a sandwich off a plate while Mrs. Munson pretended disapproval, swatting at his hand as you swat at a playful kitten, at the same time smiling and laughing at the audacity of the young man.

Mario, like Raine, had graduated from university. Mario worked as a draftsman with the New York Edison, but his passion was drawing and painting. He said his job, in a sense, was drawing. But he preferred sketching animals, flowers and people, whereas his drawings on the job were more industrial. Mario and Raine had been friends since early childhood. They had played together in the back alleys on the street where both families had lived. Prosperity had elevated both the Saijais and the De Silvas to a "better" New York address, and the parents knew each other, although there was little social contact.

Mario's father, a teacher of languages, and his mother spoke only Spanish in their home. Their sons grew up comfortable in both Spanish and English and with no accent. Mr. Saijai, however, retained the full, rich body of his native language, while Mario's mother Marta not only refused to answer anyone who spoke to her in English, she also refused to speak anything other than Spanish in or outside the home. This meant that her shopping was done mostly through sign language, and a series of grunts and deep breaths, which frustrated the clerks in the shops, and had embarrassed her sons when they accompanied her as youngsters.

As Mario passed from his teens, he had often wondered why he was named Mario, since the only Marios he knew were Italian. When he broached the subject, his mother was evasive. It was only when he needed his birth certificate that he discovered that he had, in fact, been christened Miguel. He assumed his parents felt their son, the most scholarly of the three boys, would be better equipped with an Italian name since at the time that there were far more prosperous Italians in New York than there were Spaniards. Whatever the reason, the name Mario was what the oldest Saijai son was given. However, he was advised by a lawyer friend to use Miguel whenever the need arose to sign a legal document of any kind. Little did Mario know that the conflicting names would one day be a means of anguish to the wife he would choose and who would know nothing of his being christened Miguel.

⫘⫘⫘

Mrs. Saijai was prepared not to like the young lady Mario talked about constantly. Mr. Saijai reminded his wife of their son's common sense and good judgement, and told her that Mario was getting no younger and that it was time he settled on someone to spend the rest of his life with. And what did it matter whether or not she was Spanish, as long as she was decent and would make Mario a good wife? Whenever Fernando Saijai talked like that, his wife would head for the bedroom, slam the door shut, push the blanket box under the knob and fling herself on the bed, moaning and crying. Fernando would ignore her, and eventually she would emerge, remarkably clear-eyed and intact for someone who had just gone through the throes of anguish. Fernando knew his wife well.

Mario had two younger brothers—Filipe, known as Phil, and Victor. They had all been born in Spain, but only Mario had any recollection of the homeland they had left when he was barely four years old. He remembered best the grandparents who wailed and clutched at him as the family walked up the ramp onto the big ship that would take them to what his father said would surely be a life of luxury and stability.

Luxury was more elusive than stability in the Saijai family.

Although Fernando made a good wage at the university, educating three sons as he himself was educated took every last cent he made. Mario and Phil, close in age, swept sidewalks, polished fruit at Domingo's grocery store, and delivered newspapers. In this way, they were able to help out with the stretched finances in the Saijai home.

Mario, a top student, was awarded a scholarship to university, greatly easing the burden of his higher education. He landed a job at the New York Edison the week he graduated, and rose quickly to senior draftsman, a job he liked because it allowed him to put his artistic talents to use.

It was a scholarly household. The evening meal often found the sons and Fernando deep in political discussions or dissecting the works of the great writers. Mario was especially fond of O. Henry's writings. Although the author had died in the early 1900s, his short stories were still being printed in New York papers and he was still being referred to as the prose laureate of Manhattan Island. Fernando Saijai thought O. Henry was a fly-by-night who would soon be forgotten. Mario would argue that he wrote of the common man and that one day he would be remembered as one of America's great masters of the short story. And so the talk around the Saijai table would be stimulating and often heated, and always above Marta's head. Which was the way it should be, according to Fernando, who grew up in a household where the women were necessary, but not necessarily equal.

Chapter Eleven

"¿Quién es esa señorita? ¿No es de nuestra religión?" Marta Saijai was wringing her hands in the kitchen. Fernando's frame filled the doorway to the dining room, his fists planted firmly on his hips, squaring off with his wife of thirty years. "What does it matter if she is not of our faith? She is, after all, a Catholic. And a good one too, Mario has said. Marta, our son's happiness is all that matters. I like Mabs very much. She has a good mind, and she loves Mario. Should not that be our only concern?"

Marta came a step closer to her husband and lowered her voice. "Entonces, espera llegar a ser enfermera. ¿Estás seguro?"

"Of course I'm sure she wants to be a nurse. Hasn't Raine told us how he watches her at her duties in Hackensack Hospital and how he is impressed with her? Please, Marta, do not make this difficult for our son. Mario deserves our love and our acceptance of Mabs." Fernando turned and followed the sound of laughter and happy voices to the large room at the front of the house. All the young people were there. Mario and his brothers, Raine, Rosie and Mabs. They were talking excitedly about their visit to the Metropolitan Art Museum. Mario had been thrilled with the recently acquired Egyptian Collection of the Tomb of Perneb. The museum had made massive alterations to accommodate the showing, and Mario's bent for drawing had him redesigning the display on graph paper on the parlour floor.

"See how much better it would have been had consideration been given to lighting," he said. Mabs was impressed with the keen enthusiasm he had for anything to do with art. She was eager to learn everything there was to know about the things that interested him. Mario had picked up a pamphlet on the museum and the Perneb collection, and Mabs had tucked it into her purse. The next time they went to the museum, Mabs would be just as knowledgeable as the rest of them.

Marta came to the parlour door and saw the young people, some sitting cross-legged on the floor, the rest occupying the big velvet settee. The young woman in question sat primly in the low slipper chair, ankles crossed, skirt modestly covering her legs. Marta would do her best to accept this new friend in Mario's life. She was certainly more presentable than the last one he had brought home. Perhaps Fernando was right. At any rate, Mario was her son, and his happiness was more important than her prejudices.

Marta motioned everyone to come to the table. She managed a smile and made eye contact with this young woman with the rather undignified name of Mabs. But she would talk to Mario when they were alone. That was her right. After all, she was Mario's mother. Marta had gone to extra care in preparing the meal. She was justly proud of her talents in the kitchen, and the table was laden with chicken dishes, rice flavoured with azafran, and small cakes iced with sugar and almonds.

The house was quiet. The young people had gone. Fernando had retired to his study to go over the next day's lessons. Filipe and Victor, sharing a room on the second floor, had settled in for the night, aware of the early morning classes that would take them out of the house by eight o'clock. Mario sat at one end of the cleared dining table with graph paper in front of him and a little mound of honed pencils sticking out of a cup.

Marta wiped the table again. She hummed a tuneless strain. She did that when she was either nervous or excited. Tonight she was nervous.

"Me cuesta entender por qué no has podido conocer alguna chica joven y amable que pueda hablar nuestro idioma."

Mario sighed. "You wonder why I have not been able to meet any nice young ladies who speak my language. But Mama, my language is English. Your language is Spanish," he answered in their native tongue. "It matters not to me what language Mabs speaks. She is the most wonderful girl I have ever met. I am growing very fond of her, and I pray she is growing fond of me. We have many good times together. I want you to like her, Mama. It would mean a lot to me." He reached up and took her hand and pressed it to his lips. Marta was overcome with emotion.

Of course she would learn to like Mabs. Maybe not love her. But like her she would. That was a first step. For Mario, she would do this.

Chapter Twelve

Raine and Rosie were married on a perfect fall day. The leaves had fallen in Central Park, and the air was as crisp as a piece of newly toasted bread. The wedding was small and simple, with Mrs. Vineberg weeping about the loss of a daughter to yet another man of questionable heritage. However, she never introduced Raine by his proper name thereafter; she always referred to him as "my son-in-law the doctor."

Mabs and Mario were the couple's attendants, and after the brief ceremony presided over by both a rabbi and a priest, a rare combination for the era, a light supper was served at the Hallington Hotel. The entire wedding party stood on the steps of the hotel as the couple entered a taxi for the ride to Central Station and the train that would take them away for a weekend honeymoon. Raine was able to get only two days off from his duties at Hackensack Hospital, and when they returned their half of the newly purchased house would be ready and waiting. Comments were made about the other half being empty, and Mario, in an unusual show of shyness, said that probably wouldn't be the case for long.

Unknown to anyone else in the party, Mario had proposed to Mabs and she had readily accepted. They decided not to say anything until after Rosie and Raine's wedding so as not to detract from their friends' day of celebration.

Neither Mario nor Mabs realized that the Hackensack Hospital wouldn't be as overjoyed as they were about their impending marriage. Married women were not allowed in the nursing program at the outset of training, nor were they allowed to be married during the three-year course. When Mabs approached Matron to tell her the good news, Matron showed her disappointment immediately.

"You know, Lapointe, you would be an excellent nurse. You have all the qualities we look for in the profession. Unfortunately, I have no control over the rules of the hospital. And incidentally, we are not unique; most hospitals I know do not accept married women in their programs. Of course, if you finished your nursing and then got married, that would be acceptable. I suggest you talk it over with your young man and come to a mutual decision. And, Lapointe, I am sorry. I would hate to lose you, but naturally the choice in the end must be yours."

Mabs couldn't believe what she had heard. That afternoon she went about her duties numbly. She wished she had the night off, but that wasn't to be her good fortune that day. She worked right through the evening and into the morning hours. When she finally escaped to The Hall, it was to fling herself on her cot and weep into her pillow until she fell into a sleep of exhaustion. She had almost two full years to go in her training. She was fairly sure what her decision would be, but she would talk to Mario first. He would be more rational than she was, and together they would decide what road to take.

The week stretched before her. Mario had been given an extra assignment at his office, and Mabs was on full duty until the next weekend. It was the longest seven days Mabs had ever endured. The blessing was that the hospital was busy and overcrowded, and Mabs—although Matron's news was never far from her awareness—was able to block out her anguish for some of the time as she went about the duties of a nurse-in-training.

There was a bite in the air when Mario arrived at The Hall on Sunday morning. Mabs met him in the vestibule and asked if he would mind if they went to church before they boarded the train for New York. They knelt in the big church with the oak pillars and ceiling trusses and windows of coloured glass. Mabs took her rosary from her pocket, and as she silently fingered the beads, tears began to stream down her face. Mario knew at once it wasn't the solemnity of the moment that was causing his Mabs to cry. It had to be something more serious. He lifted her by the elbow and they went out into the bright sun of the late fall day, heading for the park across the street. Mabs was in a full-fledged state of hysterics by then, and Mario, with his arm around her, eased her onto a park bench and waited for her to bring her crying under control.

She poured out her anguish, and the two clung to each other, both realizing that the decision they would come to would be the most important in their lives. "I want to be a nurse. But I want to be your wife more. This rule of the hospital makes no sense to me," Mabs sobbed.

Mario cradled her. "Mabs, I must tell you something, and this may or may not help you decide, but I must go to the recruitment office next week. It looks very much like I will be going overseas, or at the very least to a training camp far away from New York. I would like you to be my wife before I go, whether it be overseas or to camp. But you know I will never tell you what you must do. That has to be your decision. I know how much you want to graduate, and I will respect whatever you decide to do. We can marry when the war is over."

Mario thought perhaps Mabs had fallen asleep on his shoulder. There was not a word spoken for the longest while, and not a movement of muscle or limb. And then, with a great sigh, she raised her head. "I have made up my mind. I shall give up nursing. I couldn't bear to have you go off before we are married. And, Mario, I want you to know that this is my decision. You have not influenced me in any way. This is what I want to do."

A biting wind had come up in the park. A few last leaves fluttered to the ground. The big white Victorian building down the street, Mabs' home for the past year, beckoned like a mother urging her child to come in from the cold. Mabs looked at the smoke coming out of one of the chimneys, curling up into the Hackensack sky, and for a moment, only a slight moment, she regretted her decision. But then she felt the warmth of Mario's arm around her, and she knew without a doubt her determination to become Mario's wife was the right course to follow. How could she know that the decision would bring her the utmost joy, and also the most extreme anguish and pain, of her life?

Chapter Thirteen

Three days after their wedding Raine and Rosie moved into their new home. Mrs. Munson insisted on carting supper over that night to feed the newlyweds and Mario. The house was sparsely furnished, mostly with cast-offs from their parents' homes, but also with a brand new stove and icebox, gifts from the De Silvas. A small table looked tiny in the large dining room at the front of the house, and Mario joked that it was a stroke of luck that there were only four of them to sit down, because he could find only four chairs.

Mrs. Munson had brought a pot of stew, rich with vegetables and gravy. Homemade bread and a newly baked apple pie rounded out the meal. The talk was of the war, and Raine's disappointment that he hadn't been able to join up because his was considered an essential job. Mario said he would be going to the recruitment station at the end of the week. The mood was sombre. No one took this war lightly. And that went for Mrs. Munson as well, whose two nephews had already been sent to training posts outside of New York State.

A gentle tap came from the front door and then the knob turned and the door opened. Mabs, small suitcase in hand, entered the hall that opened into the dining room, and as soon as she saw the four, a flood of tears began to course down her face. Mario sprang to his feet and eased Mabs into his chair, kneeling beside her.

Her nursing career was over. She had left Hackensack Hospital. Mario had to fill in the blanks, and the others sat dumbfounded, looking from one to the other. Only then did Mario and Mabs reveal their marriage plans, and although it was joyous news, it was marred by the circumstances surrounding it.

"I'll finish out my week at the office," Mario said, "and then I will head down to the recruitment office. I had no idea, Mabs, that you would leave the hospital so soon. Are you absolutely sure you are doing the right thing?"

Mabs had worked her hanky into a twisted knot. "I've never

been more sure. I'm sorry about the tears, but this is such an emotional time for me. Being a nurse at one time was paramount, but it no longer is. I want to be married to you, Mario, and settled before you leave New York. Surely, Rosie, you can understand that. And if the hospital won't let me be married while I finish my training, then I have no other choice." Mabs looked pleadingly at Rosie for assurance.

"Mabs, you've done the right thing. I would have done exactly as you have, had I been in your position. Now, let's celebrate instead of sitting here moping."

Raine opened a bottle of wine, and everyone tried to bring an air of joviality to the evening. Mrs. Munson said Mabs could have her cot until the wedding if she wished, assuming no date had been set. However, Mario interrupted and in his usual take-charge mode said, "I see no reason why the wedding should wait, do you Mabs? We could be married before the weekend, that is unless you want to wait and have a bigger affair. The choice is yours, but it could be that I will be leaving New York by next week." When it was put that way, Mabs agreed to the plan.

And so it was decided the young couple would be married in the mayor's office as soon as Mario could make arrangements and finalize the legal end of the ceremony. Only then did the meal take on a festive note, and soon Mabs was as excited as the rest of the party, and her cheeks turned rosy, her eyes shone, and there was no doubt in her mind, not even for a second, that she had made the right decision. Mario would look after her. He would be the one who would keep her safe, and he would be the one to bring to her young life a new dimension. As she looked around at these friends who had meant so much to her, Mabs silently said a prayer of thanks. Just as Mama had said when Mabel was a little girl, "There is a master plan for each of us."

Chapter Fourteen

Marta Saijai was not happy. In fact, she was devastated. It would be hard to determine which upset her more, the fact that Mario was signing up to go to war, or the fact that he and Mabs had been married, unknown to anyone in the family. They had come around to the Saijai home immediately after the ceremony. Fernando put his arms around his son, and wished him well, and warmly welcomed Mabs into the family. Marta, close to tears, stood aside and wrung her hands, and looking from one to another tried desperately to bring some sense to what had happened. "Why did you not tell us? If this is such a joyful occasion could we not have been part of it?" Although Mabs had no idea what Mrs. Saijai was saying, she knew it was about her. She could see the disappointment on her mother-in-law's face, and she wondered if she would ever be able to break through the barrier the older woman had built against her.

Mario gently took his mother's hands in his. "Mama, there is so little time, and none of us knows what the future holds. We want you to be happy for us. For the sake of all of us, I ask that you welcome Mabs just as Papa has done. She is a wonderful woman, and it will mean so much to me if I know she is being accepted by both my parents."

Marta would never be fully accepting of anyone her Mario chose for a wife. When Fernando moved his family from Spain, it was with great reluctance that Marta had left her homeland, and she clung to her children as if they were a lifeline thrown to her at sea. She had never fully adjusted to life in New York. Mario often wondered whether, if his father had chosen a smaller city, and if his mother had made an attempt to learn English, she would have been happier. At any rate, Mario had a wife now, and he would do everything he could to bring together the two women who meant most to him. It would be an uphill climb, he knew, but he was sure in his heart his mother would accept Mabs and be thankful one day that he had chosen a wife who would be a kind and considerate daughter-in-law, and a good wife and mother.

The young couple moved immediately into the other half of the house Mario had bought jointly with Raine. Like the De Silvas' apartment, there was little furniture, but the day after the wedding Mario and Mabs bought the essentials to make housekeeping manageable, and Mario immediately opened a bank account so that Mabs could furnish the home as she wished. Mabs depended heavily on Rosie, and the day Mario headed off to the recruitment station, the two newly married girls headed out to shop for staples to fill the pantry.

President Woodrow Wilson had taken the United States into the war on April 6, 1917, more than six months before Mabs' and Mario's wedding. A few days before that, the entire country read his address to Congress in every daily newspaper across the United States. Although Mario thought the president had moved too slowly to join the Allies, he was nevertheless impressed with Wilson's speech. He had clipped it out of the *Times*, and the morning he headed to the recruiting office he took the piece of paper out of his pocket and read it again. It had been in his pocket for months. He stood in the hallway and with the light of the cold, crisp autumn morning coming through the door pane, he unfolded the paper and read it again.

"It is a fearful thing to lead this great peaceful people into war, into the most terrible and disastrous of all wars....But the right is more precious than peace, and we shall fight for the things which we have always carried nearest our hearts—for democracy...for the rights and liberties of small nations, for a universal domination of right by such a concert of free peoples as shall bring peace and safety to all nations and make the world itself at last free." As always, when Mario read Wilson's address, he became emotional. With mixed feelings of patriotism and apprehension, this was the day he would answer his president's call.

Mario believed it was the German government's stand that it would sink every vessel that approached Great Britain, Ireland or Mediterranean ports that finally pushed the President of the United States into his decision to enter the war. Shortly after that address that took the United States into the world war, the government had declared that all men between the ages of 21 and 30 would register for service. The names would be put in the jury wheel, with the intention that of the ten million names, 500,000 would be recruited. Mario's office had tried to influence him to wait for his call, but Mario wanted to enlist as soon as the New York Edison had a replacement for him. Months passed and it was soon apparent that his superiors had done little to recruit someone to fill Mario's chair.

He gave his notice the same week he was married, and it was only a few days later, on a brisk fall morning, with the bite of an early winter in the air, that Mario caught a bus at his corner and headed down to the heart of the city. Mabs and Rosie had a full day ahead of them, what with getting staples for the cupboard, and buying linens for both new homes. They planned a joint dinner that night. Raine would be home from the hospital by six, and Mario whenever he finished having his tests and medical examination at the recruiting office. For both young brides, it was a joyous time, in spite of the shadow of Mario's leaving. Their friendship had held for six years, and Mabs knew that without Rosie, she probably would have packed up and gone back to Canada long ago.

Rosie's appearance had changed little in that time. Marriage had given her a mature look that belied her young years. She kept up with the latest fashions, and although never extravagant, she wanted Raine to be proud of her. Coming into the marriage with what Rosie thought was a decided disadvantage—a lack of formal education added to a Jewish background—she was determined to prove herself a suitable wife for an up-and-coming doctor. The De Silvas took an instant liking to their new daughter-in-law, and Mrs. De Silva opened her home to Rosie and made sure she met some other young women in the Gramercy Park area. The senior De Silvas had lived there long enough to be accepted as suitable residents of the mainly upper-class, close-knit community.

As well, the De Silvas thought highly of Mario's new bride. Mabs had grown in height over the past six years, now standing about 5' 8" tall, "standing on a pail," as Mario would say. She still was a good half foot shorter than her husband. Mabs had inherited her mother's jet black hair and clear skin, and the Lapointe eyes, large and clear and the colour of rich walnuts. Both girls loved to laugh, and even the simplest pleasure filled them with joy and a feeling of well-being. They found happiness in a simple walk through Central Park, feeding the pigeons, browsing through Wanamaker's Department Store, and stopping for hot chocolate or coffee in Lord and Taylor's Coffee Shop.

Mario's leaving was never far from Mabs' mind, but on that particular day in the fall of 1917, Mabs felt in the very depths of her being that she couldn't have been happier and more content. Nursing was behind her, and although she would have had an immense feeling of accomplishment had she graduated, she nonetheless, on that cold fall day, knew that she had traded a profession for something far more valuable and long-lasting. She would make the Saijais proud of her, and surely eventually Marta

Saijai would accept her and realize that her daughter-in law's only mission was to make her son happy.

Chapter Fifteen

Rosie had splurged and bought a bunch of fall flowers from the vendor at the corner. With Mabs' help, she had created a festive atmosphere in the De Silva apartment. The dishes were new, a gift from Raine's aunt who, rumour had it, had more money than she knew what to do with. And since Raine was her favourite nephew, she found great joy in bestowing on him and his new bride not only a set of Rosenthal china, but a complete eight-place setting of sterling silver as well.

Raine was home, earlier than he had anticipated, and Mario was yet to return from the enlistment office. Outside it had started to rain, and icy needles were pounding against the dining room window. Raine lit the gas fireplace, however, and soon the room was warm and cozy.

The three friends sat on the davenport in the parlour, chatting easily. More than once Rosie let out a long, contented sigh. Raine assured Mabs, who was getting anxious that Mario had yet to return, that signing up was not just a matter of putting your name to a sheet of paper and being told when and where to appear. "There are tests and more tests. Especially since Mario will likely be earmarked for something a bit higher than an ordinary enlisted man, because of his education and present position at the Edison," he explained.

And then Mario was there. His coat was slick with rain and his black hair flat against his forehead. He was as sober as Mabs had ever seen him. She thought the worst. "He is going to be shipped out immediately. Why else would he be wearing such a look of concern?" Raine took the wet coat and hung it on the back of a chair near the fireplace, and handed Mario a glass of red wine. They waited for Mario to speak. When he did, it was with great hesitation, as if he didn't quite know how to begin.

"I have been rejected. I was the longest time working my way to the head of the line-up, first of all. It seemed to me that half of New York had beaten me to the recruitment office. And then the testing began. The army doctor was the most belligerent man I have ever seen." Trying to bring humour to what he had said, he added, "Raine, if you turn out like that, I shall disown you."

"Why have you been turned down?" Raine looked anxious; he got up from his seat and went to stand beside Mario, putting a hand on his shoulder.

"I have something wrong with my heart. The doctor said it isn't terribly serious, but serious enough to keep me out of the services. Here, Raine, I asked him to write it down so that I could discuss it with you."

Mabs was chalk white and could only stare at her new husband as if it was the first time she had ever laid eyes on him. "But you aren't sick, Mario. You have always been so healthy and full of energy. Surely there is a mistake," she said, choking on every word.

Everyone looked to Raine for assurance. He refolded the paper and handed it back to Mario. "What you have is not that uncommon. It just means your heart misses the occasional beat. I can see why it would stop them from accepting you in the army, but I can assure you, you will live a long and healthy life. The only danger would be if you caught a severe illness, like pneumonia or something like that. You must be careful, that's all."

"I'm not concerned one iota about the heart problem. I am concerned about not being able to join my country in this war," Mario said. Mabs looked to Raine for reassurance, which he gave by grinning from ear to ear and then reaching down and taking Mario's hand and hoisting him out of his chair.

"Well, aren't we a pair. Both rejects. Me, because they think I am needed here, and you because your ticker misses a beat! Well, let's eat. I'm ravenous, and Mario, this little heart problem isn't going to do a thing to your appetite. You'll still be able to eat all of us under the table. What does surprise me is that it hasn't been picked up before."

The four showed different emotions during the meal. Raine was obviously not unhappy that his best friend was not going off to war. Mabs was ecstatic that Mario was being spared as well, and she would just put the heart problem out of her mind and look after Mario and make sure he was kept fit and well. Rosie felt the same as Mabs. The four young people had much living to do, and they would be doing it together. Mario, although dejected, seemed not to be concerned about his newly discovered medical problem. And by the time the evening was over, fortified by several glasses of wine and Rosie's good dinner, Mario accepted his fate and decided he would go back to the New York Edison in the morning, where he was sure his job would be waiting for him.

Chapter Sixteen

Mabs felt the winters in New York were colder than those she had left in Canada. Of course, they weren't. But the dampness of the city chilled her bones, and even the gas fireplace in the dining room failed to take the cold out of the room when she served the evening meal. The dampness did nothing, however, to abate the sheer joy and contentment she found in her new role as wife to

Mario. Mario went back to his old job as if he had never left, even to the point of being given the same desk in the same corner of the second-floor office. In time he was able to put behind him the terrible disappointment of being left behind while co-workers and friends went off to the war. Certainly the prospect of spending his free time with his new wife was a happy one. He gave little thought to his newly discovered heart ailment, and with assurance from Raine, Mabs too was convinced that although it was indeed something to be aware of, the skipped heartbeat would do little to affect Mario's longevity.

Rosie had learned to sew at a young age, mainly out of necessity but also because her father was employed in the garment industry, where he was often given bundles of left-over material and threads to take home. She tried to teach Mabs the art of making some of her own clothes. It was soon obvious to both that Mabs' talents lay elsewhere, although that didn't stop Mabs from trying. Raine's rich aunt bought a wonderful sewing machine for Rosie and she created velvet drapes for the parlour, made pillow covers for the davenport and even ventured into upholstering, at which she was less successful. Nonetheless, Rosie and Mabs spent many hours in the De Silva half of the house, the click-clack of the sewing machine mingling with their giggles. It was a wonderful time in the lives of the two girls.

Christmas in 1917 was the first of many the two couples would celebrate together. Rosie, raised in an Orthodox Jewish home, adapted to the customs of her Christian husband and his family, and seemed to take more delight in the Christmas tree and presents than did her in-laws. They, of course, were thrilled.

Mabs, ever mindful of her four brothers and father back in Ottawa, and urged on by Mario, prepared a large box of presents and sent it off by train. Louis and Herby, of course, were still overseas, but the Christmas tags emphatically stated that their presents were to be kept for their return. And for young Amby and Henry, there were books on New York, puzzles and dress shirts. For Papa there were new grey felt spats with shiny black button closings, and a paisley Ascot tie.

Mario introduced Mabs to the opera and Carnegie Hall, and Broadway productions and readings at the city library. She developed a fondness for the works of Ralph Waldo Emerson, and vowed if she ever had a son, she would name him in the poet's honour. Mario bought her Emerson's complete works for Christmas that year, and promised her that some day he would take her to Concord, Massachusetts to the Sleepy Hollow Cemetery where Emerson was buried in 1882.

Although she wasn't, and never would be, an expert seamstress, Mabs was quite adept at embroidery. She made fancy pillows and needleworked some of her favourite Emerson poems on their fronts, and these she scattered throughout the house. She made a special one for Mario's mother, which seemed to please her mother-in-law, and went a long way towards convincing her that there was more to her son's wife than a pleasant face and a regal stature.

In fact, Marta Saijai began to accept Mabs more and more, and although she had yet to take the young couple up on any of their invitations to visit and have a meal, she did include them often in special dinners and family celebrations at the Saijai home. Mario said that in time, his mother would come around. Mabs was not as optimistic as her husband.

Of more concern was the accelerating war. Mabs kept in constant touch with her father in Ottawa, and each time a letter arrived from him, her hands shook as she opened it, fearing that she would learn something terrible had happened to one of her brothers. Mabs tried to picture them in uniform, but all she could see in her mind's eye were the young boys she had left behind an eternity ago. She prayed over her rosary, and attended the big Catholic Church in the neighbourhood, and lit candles, asking God to keep her brothers safe. In her naiveté, she felt that if she lived a good life and prayed a lot, Louis and Herby would be brought home safely.

The winter passed quickly for Mabs and Mario. There was much to do, and many new places to discover. Mabs was on a mission of learning, and she absorbed knowledge as a towel absorbs water. By spring, Rosie and Raine were expecting their first child. The senior De Silvas were overjoyed, and the wealthy aunt began sending parcels around by taxi almost daily. Spring erupted early, and Central Park blossomed under the warm skies. Mabs was almost as thrilled over Rosie's pregnancy as were the De Silvas. Now she had another prayer to add to her long list. "Keep Rosie safe and may she have a healthy baby," and then she would add: "and if it is your will, may I too soon have some news to tell Mama and Papa Saijai."

The year 1918 was to be an eventful one, not only for the Saijais and the De Silvas, but also for the city of New York. The Board of Education was asked to ban all teaching of German in the high schools. Although there were many people of German descent in the city, most had never been any further than the Burroughs of New York. Some anglicized their names to fit in with the changing attitudes. Many others wondered how they could be blamed for a war that was happening thousands of miles away. Membership at the Deutscher Verein club, housed in a beautiful Romanesque structure built entirely of Indiana limestone, catered to the German population, and Mario and Mabs often walked by its impressive doorway on their way to the Catholic Club where they had memberships. Mario used the Catholic Club's extensive library, and when the two would pass the Deutscher Verein, Mario would comment on the senselessness of war, and how conflict could separate friends and build animosities where none should exist.

"Otto Springer and I used to work together, but he has the misfortune of having a grandfather who came here from Germany before he was born. He has lost his job because of a war he had nothing to do with starting," he would say. Mabs would wonder how Mario could defend someone like Otto Springer, and at the same time show such regret and pain at not being able to fight in the war between Germany and the United States. However, she kept her thoughts to herself. Mario was much more clever than she, and she had seen him and Raine in heated debate, not only over the war, but on issues like the increase in traffic on the streets of New York, which according to the *New York Times* had grown to the unenviable distinction of having the world's heaviest traffic.

As for Mabs, she loved the increase in motor vehicles on the streets, the crowded elevated trains, the buses packed with people in transit to and from their jobs, and the throngs of shoppers in her favourite department stores. In a few short years, Mabs had grown from a frightened young immigrant from Canada running an elevator, to a homemaker whose days were filled with learning and adventure. In the summer of 1918, she and Mario had their portrait taken at Giovanni's. It showed a handsome young man with piercing dark eyes, and a young matron with a confident smile and a cameo face framed by marcelled hair and arched brows, all above a fashionably huge starched white collar standing high at the back of her head like a cardboard sign. Mabs looked at the picture, and decided Papa should have a copy. He would see a great change in his daughter, and it would be the first glimpse he would have of the son-in-law whom Mabs had written so much about.

New York that summer was hot and humid. Rosie lumbered about and spent a lot of time sitting on the front stoop which was shaded by a huge elm tree. Mabs would sit beside her, fanning her friend with a folded newspaper. The baby's room was ready, and it was already decided that Mario and Mabs would be godparents when it was time to have him christened. Rosie knew in her heart she was carrying a boy. Raine was sure it was going to be a girl. Both predicted correctly, when Rosie delivered twins the day before the war ended in November.

Chapter Seventeen

The twins, Martha and Joseph, were four years old when Mabs rushed into the duplex next door to tell Rosie she was sure she was pregnant. "I fell against the sink this morning. And all I was doing was brushing my teeth. Rosie, I was so dizzy, I could barely make it to the bed. And my stomach is churning, and I just know it isn't influenza." Mabs' cheeks were flaming, and Rosie had to force her into a chair to tell her to settle down. "A sick stomach can be from any number of things—the oysters we ate last night, for instance. Mabs, don't get your hopes up again. Let's wait and see what happens."

They decided not to say anything to Mario and Raine until they had more evidence that Mabs was indeed carrying a baby. They had been disappointed before. But as the winter weather escalated, and Mabs' symptoms continued, she could no longer conceal her excitement, and Raine confirmed that indeed Mabs could expect a baby sometime in June. There was great celebration and the senior Saijais joined in the anticipation with great happiness. This would be the first grandchild for both Marta and Fernando and for John Louis

Lapointe. Mabs wasted no time, as soon as her pregnancy was confirmed, in writing to Papa to tell him her wonderful news. Mario added a note to the bottom of the letter asking for Papa's blessing.

The months ahead were easy ones for Mabs, in spite of the fact that she grew to an enormous size by the end of her sixth month. She had trouble climbing the stairs, and waddled like a duck when she walked, but the sheer joy of impending motherhood cancelled out any discomfort she experienced. Rosie loaned her a crib that the twins had outgrown, and a small room at the top of the stairs was readied for the expected baby.

Mabs decided she wanted her baby to be born at the Hackensack Hospital. Raine promised he would be there with her, putting her mind at ease.

In the small hours of a humid June night, several weeks after what Raine expected to be her due date, Mabs was admitted to the Hackensack Hospital. Her delivery was surprisingly easy. Especially when Raine came in to tell her that her new son had weighed fourteen pounds, eleven and a half ounces. He was the largest baby ever born in the hospital, and everyone including the cleaning staff and the women from the laundry came up to the nursery to view this newborn, who one doctor said looked big enough to be enrolled in school!

Before the day was out, Mabs had declared he would be called Emerson after her favourite poet, and his second name would be John after his grandfather in Ottawa.

Mabs had been around Rosie and her twins often enough that she slipped into the role of motherhood with ease. Emerson was a happy baby with black eyes and hair the colour of red bricks. He seemed to be constantly smiling or laughing out loud, beginning when he was several months old, and his proud father was therefore convinced that he had spawned a genius.

Mabs took many pictures of her new son, and sent them off to her father. Her brothers, after returning from the war, had found jobs, and there was talk that Louis might come to New York with the marble company he had gone to work for when he had shed his uniform. Mario could see how happy that would make Mabs, and he suggested Louis could live with them until he found his own quarters.

Young Emerson, everyone agreed, was growing "like a weed". He walked at an early age and showed signs of having a mind of his own. Mabs had to watch him constantly. He was found turning on the gas in the fireplace, flushing a towel down the toilet, which necessitated a visit from a plumber, and, one day, stuffing his teddy bear in the oven with the roast. His antics seemed to be an indication of what Mabs and Mario could expect when he was older. Little did they know that not only would he grow up to be clever and artistic like his father, he would also develop into a mischievous young boy who had everyone wondering how he would ever reach adulthood.

In the meantime, Emerson was cherished and loved, and doted on by his grandparents. His hair had turned a bright red, and his cheeks were covered with freckles, both of which added to his impish look, and endeared him to everyone who met him.

When Emerson was five years old, Mario and Mabs enrolled him in a day school close to their home. He was bright and full of energy. Belleville Academy was a small school run by a young woman who came from England and who had once tutored children connected with the Royal Family, although she stopped short of saying they were actually princes and princesses. Nonetheless, Mario was impressed with her credentials (especially since she said Emerson had obviously inherited his father's artistic talent) and she soon had the young boy doing sketches and paintings which he brought home by the dozen.

Just before Emerson's fifth birthday, Mabs found out she was again pregnant. Both she and Mario were overjoyed. Perhaps it would be a girl this time.

All that summer, Mabs kept telling Rosie she had a feeling of impending doom, as if perhaps something was destined to go wrong with this long-awaited second pregnancy. Rosie blamed it on one of the hottest summers on record. Mabs told herself Rosie was right, and by August, she agreed that the weather had a great deal to do with her feelings. The young couples tried to get relief on the back verandah in the evenings, while their children slept in airless rooms upstairs. Suddenly, at the end of September, relief came. The weather got cooler.

Mario came from the office one night, pounding through the door, rushing to the back of the house, and showing such excitement that Mabs could only look in amazement. He was talking so fast Mabs had to reach out and take his arm and tell him to slow down, that she had no idea what he was talking about.

"I have been offered a commission to Paris. General Dynamics is building a subsidiary office over there, and I've been working with their architects for months. There is to be a large rotunda, and they want me to do the artwork for it. My office has agreed to give me a leave of absence for three years, which is what they estimate to be the time I will need. Mabs, what an opportunity this will be. At first I said no, I couldn't possibly leave my family." He paused to take a breath. "They said they expected me to take my family for the next three years. Mabs, what an opportunity this will be for all of us!"

Mabs was so stunned she just stared at her husband. "But what about the new baby? When do we have to go? Mario, there are so many questions on my mind. Shouldn't we think about it for a while?"

"Mabs, there is no time. We have to be there by the end of next month." Mario steered Mabs to a chair in the parlour. "Now, this is my thought. You will have to agree, of course, or we will decide on other options. I understand a child is a citizen of the country in which it is born. Naturally, you will want the baby to be an American citizen. I am suggesting I go on ahead, and then when the baby comes, you, Emerson and our new one will join me."

Mabs could see how excited Mario was. She knew too this was a rare opportunity for him. She could find no fault with the plan. Especially since her baby would be born in Hackensack Hospital. And so within a few hours, having brought the De Silvas in from next door to share their news, they put in motion the wheels of the move.

They would sell their furniture and rent their half of the house with a three-year lease. Mabs would book passage for January or February to join Mario in Paris. The baby would be two months old by then, and Raine was sure, if it was healthy, and he was confident it would be, there would be no concern over the voyage.

The De Silvas even offered Mabs accommodations from the time the furniture was sold until it came time to sail. Rosie and Mabs wept at the thought of their separation, but everyone agreed it would be a wonderful and enriching experience for the young family.

Mario was so busy getting ready to go, training someone to take his place at the Edison, and getting everyone's papers in order, that he had little time to help Mabs clear out the duplex. Raine warned Mario to slow down. He was working too hard, and not taking time to rest, and if he didn't watch out he would be exhausted when it came time for him to sail at the end of October. But Mario paid little attention. There was much to do, and very little time to do it in.

The furniture sold quickly, and the week before Mario was ready to leave New York, the young family moved next door with their friends, occupying a back bedroom. The last few days passed quickly and happily, even though most evenings Mario went back to the office to finalize plans for his transfer and work on plans for the new structure in Paris. He was exhausted, but Mabs was sure she had never seen him happier.

The day of his departure the air was crisp and clear. Mario had to be wakened after falling into bed at midnight, so tired he hardly knew where he was. The cold that he had contracted was worse, but Raine said many days on ship, relaxing and enjoying the salt sea air, would be like a tonic.

Rosie offered to see that Emerson got off to school, and while the sun was still low in the east, Mabs and Mario climbed into a taxi. Mario's luggage had been boarded the night before. The dock was crowded and Mario had to elbow his way past the mobs to get to the ramp. Mabs, huge and awkward, held tightly to his hand. Mario's cough was deep, and worrisome to Mabs, but before she knew it Mario was gone from her view. She saw him briefly at the rail, and she watched as he motioned her to go ahead home. He turned and left, and Mabs saw him cough into his handkerchief.

She had her rosary in her pocket, and she fingered the beads. Her legs were numb from her weight, and she suddenly realized she hadn't worn enough clothes to keep warm at the docks, and so she turned to the taxi that Mario had ordered to wait. She put her head back on the seat and slept soundly until the driver gently tapped her on the shoulder and said, "Lady, you're home."

Mabs with brother Lou in New York circa 1925

Mario and Emerson, Easter Sunday, Bronx Park, NY

Mario's co-workers at the New York Edison. His desk can be seen in the foreground.

Mario and son Emerson. Notice Emerson's "Canada" hat. A gift from Uncle Lou?

A young Emerson

Chapter Eighteen

The kindest thing the De Silvas could have done for Mabs was to invite her into their home to live out the few months before she too would head out to Paris to join Mario, and this they did. Even at that, she was more lonely than she had ever been in her life. Emerson too kept asking where his Dada was. Finally Raine took out a map of the world and spread it out on the dining room table, and together they charted the crossing of the Atlantic, marking the route with thumb tacks. After the first two nights Emerson accepted that his father was going a long way, and soon his mother would be going far away too, and they would all meet again in a wonderful city on the other side of the ocean.

It was on the third day, when Mabs and Rosie were lingering over their afternoon tea, that a gentle knock came to the front door. Rosie came back with a long envelope and handed it to Mabs. "This is a radio-gram for you. I signed for it."

Mabs' first thought was of Papa in Ottawa. "Oh, Rosie, I'm scared to open it."

She shoved it across the table in Rosie's direction. It was in a long beige-coloured envelope. Rosie opened it and unfolded the single sheet of paper from inside.

She read it first herself, and as soon as she looked up Mabs knew there was terrible news.

"It's Papa, isn't it?"

"No. It isn't. Do you want me to read it to you? I'm so sorry, Mabs. It's terrible news. Maybe you should read it yourself."

Mabs shook her head, as if in doing so she could either delay or erase entirely what was inside the radio-gram.

Rosie cleared her throat several times, and already her eyes were welling with tears. "Mrs. Saijai. Stop. We sincerely regret to inform you that Miguel Saijai, who came on board with a severe cold, developed pneumonia. Stop. He succumbed to the disease in spite of the most valiant attempts of our doctor to save him. Stop. He was buried at sea. His personal belongings will be coming to you on our arrival back in New York. Stop. Please accept my deepest sympathy. Stop. Captain Jacques Françoise."

Mabs clutched at her throat and her swollen belly, and pulled at her hair. "Oh, Rosie, it isn't our Mario. It has to be somebody else. There must have been a Miguel Saijai on the same trip. Mario is Mario. I have never heard of Miguel. Oh, thank God. It's someone else. Of course, I pain for whoever his family is, but I know it's not Mario. I have no idea who this Miguel is."

Rosie reached across the table to steady Mab's hands. "Mabs. Raine told me years ago that Mario's christened name was Miguel. He has been called Mario unofficially since he was a young man. No one ever knew exactly why. But all of his legal documents would have to be signed Miguel. I am so sorry, Mabs, but I must tell you that it is Mario. I wish with all my heart that I could bear this pain for you. I will call Raine at once. He will come home to be with you. We will be here for you and Emerson and your unborn child. It will be the hardest thing you will ever have to go through, but Mabs, you are strong, and for the sake of your children, you must carry on. Mario would want that."

Mabs sat at the table, stone-like. Dry-eyed. Unbelieving. Soon Emerson would be home from school. Dinner. She should make dinner. And the laundry...perhaps she should do some laundry. Her eyes darted frantically around the room. What should she do first? She went to the bedroom to get a pinny. There in the corner were the bags she and Mario had packed, ready for the trip to Paris. When her eyes rested on Mario's art cases, his easel wrapped in cardboard, only then did she accept the terrible reality of what had happened and the twist her life had taken. And only then did she give way to her tears. She fell on the bed, and sobbed, and prayed that she could handle what lay ahead for her and her children. She had little money, only the few dollars Mario had left in the bank account. Raine would help her reach decisions. He would help her decide what was best for her, Emerson and her unborn baby. She knew there could be nothing more heartbreaking than what she was going through at that very moment. She knew, too, that Mario would expect her to carry on. He would expect her to be mother and father to her babies. Surely, once she could make herself accept the terrible reality of what had happened, she would have to look ahead. It would be up to her to make a life for her children without a father. Little did Mabs know as she stared at the ceiling in the bedroom that her life was to take a twist that would alter forever the future of her children, and bring her to the very edge of despair.

Chapter Nineteen

Ten years later, if someone had asked Mabs who had made the decision that she leave New York, she wouldn't be able to say. All she could remember were those terrible cold fall days of anguish, facing the reality that Mario was gone forever, and that the full responsibility of raising two young children was hers alone.

She bathed, she dressed, she ate only when someone put a plate in front of her, she listened to voices around her, hearing little. It was Raine who finally took charge. He suggested perhaps this would be a good time for Mabs to go back to Ottawa to visit her father and four brothers. Louis had settled in New York after the war ended, and he had told Mabs time and again how very much Papa wanted to see her and Emerson. He too agreed with Raine, the time had come to go home for a visit. Then the new baby could be born in Canada and become a Canadian citizen. And when Mabs wanted to, she could return to New York.

Mabs, with only limited funds to her name, reluctantly accepted the train ticket from Louis. Although no one had talked over her return with her father, she boarded the train in New York Central one day when the trees were bare and the days were short and cold. Emerson was the only one excited about the trip. Rosie wept and promised they would meet again soon. Raine pushed money into Mabs' pocket, and Louis assured her Papa would be thrilled to have her home for a visit, and that he would send Papa a telegram immediately to let him know her time of arrival.

The Ottawa Union Station was almost empty when Mabs got off the train and entered the waiting room. It was late at night, and Emerson had to be carried by a porter. Mabs was uncomfortable from the long sit; she felt as if she was ready to go into labour at any moment.

Papa hugged her and took Emerson into his arms and ruffled his hair. "Doesn't look much like a Lapointe, does he?" he said. He had a taxi waiting at the back entrance of the station, and Mabs gratefully fell into the back seat. There was a light skiff of snow on the streets, and Mabs realized she had no overshoes for either herself or Emerson, and no money to buy them. The old tenement house hadn't changed in all the years Mabs had been away. The smell of gas still filled the back shed, and the old creton couch in the kitchen was in exactly the same corner as it was when Mabs had last seen her mother. The cushions were the same, the rocking chair beside it still had the tip of one rocker broken off, and the little pantry Mabs had called her bedroom was still a dark hole at the end of the kitchen.

Papa had a pot of green tea simmering on the back of the stove. The flat was eerily quiet. Herby and Amby had moved after the war, and Henry, Mabs knew from Papa's last letter, worked on a farm south of Ottawa. Mabs asked about Henry's wife who had been in the Royal Ottawa Sanatorium, having contracted tuberculosis when their little boy Earl was only a toddler.

"Grace is not well. And of course, Henry isn't allowed to take Earl into the san. I think she would show great improvement if she could see her son. However, there is nothing we can do to change that."

John Lapointe carried Mabs' bags into the back bedroom where her brothers had slept and brought extra blankets from the closet in the front hall. Emerson was already asleep when she laid him under the covers, and as she undressed herself, her feelings were a mixture of sadness and relief. She was sure she would never experience joy in living again. And yet she would soon have two children to raise. Because all of the money she and Mario had saved and realized from the selling of the furniture in New York had gone with him on the ship so that he could buy an aparment in Paris, Mabs had been left with only a small amount of money. Worse still, Mario's personal effects had been limited to his watch, pieces of personal identification and clothing; no money had been included in the bundle and no one connected with the ship line seemed to have any answers to her questions. She tried to consider her options, but she knew they were few. At least she had a roof over her head at Papa's. She could take time and think about what she could do to make a living for herself and her children when she got rested up and returned to New York. In the meantime, she could run Papa's house and cook meals, and do the washings. It would be less than a month until her baby was to be born, and with that thought, she fell into a deep sleep. When she wakened in the morning, Papa had already left for work. She felt rested, but still the apprehension of what lay ahead occupied her mind as she reacquainted herself with the home she had left seventeen years ago.

Chapter Twenty

The Number 2 Firehall was still next door to the tenement house and the rowdy laughter of the firemen could still be heard from the flat. But now, Mabs noticed, the horse-drawn fire engines had been replaced with shiny red trucks, and two of them always sat on the tarmac in front of the closed doors at the ready.

That December morning, with a new snowfall and a wind that went right through to her bones, Mabs took the broom and swept off the back step leading into the shed, aware of a dull ache in her back which she blamed on lifting Emerson out from behind the divan where he had hidden so he wouldn't have to eat his breakfast.

Within the hour the pain had reached her stomach, and waves of searing agony wrapped themselves around her body. She fed Emerson into his heavy clothes, put her coat on, hurried as fast as her body would let her across the yard and in the side door of the firehall.

Fire Chief Wiggins, a long-time friend of her father, jumped up from the round table where he and other firemen were playing cards.

"Hospital. Please. Get me to the Grace Hospital."

Two firemen helped Mabs climb up onto one of the fire engines outside, and another took Emerson by the hand and led him to the back of the firehall where he was soon engrossed in studying the swivel chair at the Captain's desk. With the bells ringing and the horn blowing, Chief Wiggins careened down the street with Mabs hanging on for dear life. The fire engine skidded to a halt on the snow-covered pavement in front of the Grace Hospital, where it soon became obvious someone back at the firehall had alerted them to the emergency about to arrive on their doorstep, because a group of nurses with a gurney was at the door waiting.

By mid-afternoon, Mabs had delivered a healthy baby girl, whom she decided to name Mary after her mother. Her middle name would be Gloria. Although John Lapointe came to see her in the hospital, he turned down the offer to go to the nursery window and look in at his new granddaughter. In fact, he was already hinting to Mabs that perhaps the kindest thing she could do for this new baby would be to consider giving her up for adoption. "There are many good young families who would be glad to have an infant. Families where there would be two parents. Think about it, Mabel. You must consider the welfare of your child above your own."

The idea of giving up her and Mario's baby repulsed Mabs. She would manage somehow. She asked Papa to bring her rosary to the hospital. She would pray for a solution. Surely there was some way she would be able to keep her two children and provide for them. But the hospital, she felt, was not the place to worry about it. She was exhausted and still aching with loneliness for Mario. When she got back to Papa's on Lyon Street, she would then think of what to do. In the meantime, Mary, although not as big a baby at birth as was Emerson, weighed a hefty nine and a half pounds and was gaining steadily. She, too, had a shock of flaming red hair like her brother.

Before she left the hospital Mabs' brother Henry came in from the farm he worked on in Richmond to visit her. He said his wife was losing ground with her fight against tuberculosis. He was only able to visit her through a glass partition, and every time he went to the sanatorium, he found her thinner and he could see, although not hear, the rasping cough that shook her frail body in the other room. Young Earl, whom Mabs had never seen, was a Lapointe through and through, he told her. When Mabs mentioned that Papa thought she should give up Mary for adoption, he was as appalled as she had been. "No," he said, "she is your Christmas present."

Because she was so weak and tired, the hospital didn't release Mabs until Mary was almost three weeks old. It was between Christmas and New Year's that Mabs was taken back to Lyon Street with the baby wrapped in a car robe, and Emerson, who had not been allowed into the hospital, clutching her hand, and begging his mother to leave the baby behind. He had no intention of competing for her attention.

Since there was no crib, Papa cleared out a drawer in a dresser, put in a feather pillow wrapped in a clean sheet, and called it "the baby's new bed." He still did little to acknowledge the infant, and continued to give gentle hints that Mabel and the baby would be better off if she was given up to a loving couple.

Mabs' strength returned quickly. The baby slept well, and unless she was brought out from the bedroom and her dresser-drawer bed, no one would guess there was a baby in the house. Emerson, on the other hand, was in constant motion. Mabs had to keep a keen eye on him, and tried, not too successfully, to divert his energy into something other than going into the back bedroom where he poked the baby, trying to make her cry. He was sure if she caused enough stir, she would be promptly sent back to the hospital whence she came. Like Grandpa Lapointe, Emerson felt the baby's presence was an invasion in his territory.

Whereas Emerson's reasons were feelings of jealousy, John Lapointe's were concerns about how Mabs would be able to feed and care for two children with no income. Although he made sure she knew she was welcome to stay until she was on her feet, he also made her aware that sooner or later she would have to take charge of her life and move on.

Lacrosse was over for the winter, but since Mabs had gone to New York, John had added curling to his sporting activities, and several times a week that winter he would leave the house soon after coming home from work, saying he would have his supper at Bowles' Lunch on the way to the curling club.

Mabs continued to make the meals and keep the laundry done, and clean the house. John got to leaving money on the kitchen table so that she could buy the essentials at the corner store. As well, a farmer came in from Renfrew County two or three times a month with produce and meat. He would leave an order in the back shed, pick up the envelope John had left in the door jamb and be gone before Mabs had a chance to see him. John said Albert Haneman had been going through this routine for years, that he was dependable and honest, and that he never left less than he was paid for. Solid. That's what John Lapointe called him. "Too few like him in the world today, I can tell you," he said.

Chapter Twenty-One

The first time Mabs saw Albert Haneman was through the kitchen window on his next trip to Ottawa with produce. He was dressed for the elements. Fur hat with lugs tied under his chin. A mackinaw coat over a pair of what appeared to be bib overalls, with work pants peeking out at the ankles. His cowhide mitts covered his hands, and a pipe protruded from his mouth. His face looked small and dark skinned. He spotted Mabs in the kitchen window, nodded his head and then moved on. Mabs thought he looked awfully small and that his clothes looked too big for him. "He looks like he could use a good meal," she said to herself.

It was a Saturday, so John Lapointe was home that day. He emerged from the shed and followed Albert Haneman to the end of the lane. He was gone a long time, and Mabs wondered about his being out in the cold without his heavy coat on. When he came back in, he wore the look Mabs remembered as a little girl. It was his serious look, and Mabs wondered if the farmer had told him some bad news about his family out in Renfrew County.

"Mabel, I want to talk to you. You know I have only your welfare at heart. It seems you are intent on keeping the baby." He had yet to refer to the child by her given name. "I believe I have a solution for you, and I think it is the answer to your problem. The chances of your working in Ottawa are very slim when you have two young children." John cleared his throat, took a handkerchief out of his pocket and wiped his face which was covered with beads of sweat in spite of being out in the icy cold for half an hour.

"Albert Haneman needs someone to run his house. He is a busy farmer and is the third generation to live on his homestead. He is willing to take you and the children. It would be wonderful for young Emerson, and of course, you would still be able to keep your baby." For the first time he looked up at Mabs, who had taken a chair at the kitchen table. "He needs someone to run his house, and think of the wonderful life it would be for Emerson on the farm with animals and a school close by."

Mabs showed immediate interest. Maybe this was the solution.

Maybe her prayers had been answered after all. Fingering her rosary had not been in vain. She looked down at the baby in her arms, and over at Emerson who had taken one of his grandfather's best ties and was weaving it around a chair leg. With two children, there were few options open to her. This would be a home for them, and she wouldn't have to worry about putting food in their mouths.

"I would have to have a small salary, because the children would need things from time to time. Would this Mr. Haneman be willing to give me a few dollars a month?"

John squirmed in his chair and cast his eyes to the ceiling, drumming his fingers on the oilcloth-covered kitchen table.

"Well, I'm sure there would be a few dollars put at your disposal. But Mabel, Albert lives in a very small tight community. Deeply religious. Lutherans. Very church-going people. He could not take you just to live there as a housekeeper. There would be too much talk. Not fair to either of you. I suggested you marry for the sake of everyone concerned. The children would have a father. You would have security, and I know you would find him kind and trustworthy. Albert Haneman is one of the most honest people I know. Now, before you say no, think about your children. How can you possibly raise two young children with no home and no money?"

John Lapointe made it sound like an ideal solution. Mabs thought of it as a death sentence. And then she looked at her children and she knew Papa was right. She had very little choice if she was to give her children a home, and obviously making Lyon Street a permanent address for her, Emerson and Mary was not in her father's plans.

"Would we get to know each other first? I know nothing about him. I have only seen him through the kitchen window."

"Well…" and then there was a long pause. "Albert and I have

talked and we have decided if you are agreeable, the wedding would take place, quietly of course, on his next trip into Ottawa." Mabs was astounded at how she and her children had been discussed and decisions made without consulting her. She thought better of showing the dismay she felt. She thought of this marriage as an arrangement. "I can't do much worse," she thought.

Chapter Twenty-Two

Mabs knew if she started to cry, she wouldn't stop. The same thought crossed her mind when she felt the urge to burst out laughing. Both emotions surfaced more than once, as she drove with John Lapointe to the Lutheran church in the downtown core of the city. Albert Haneman had come to the tenement house on Lyon Street with a horse and cutter, rapped at the back door, was admitted, took off his fur cap and began twirling it in his hand. He looked Mabs up and down as if he were buying a heifer. John introduced them, and Albert reached out and shook her hand. It was ice cold, and Mabs wondered if it was because of the bitterly cold January day, or if he was nervous.

Mabs wasn't nervous. She wasn't anything. Apart from the urge to laugh or cry, she felt as if she was in someone else's body. She felt unconnected to anything or anyone. This virtual stranger was going to be her husband. She had to make the best of it; it was the only hope she had of making a home for her children. Albert Haneman looked kind. But certainly he was as far removed from Mario as dawn was to dusk, in looks and demeanor. Whereas Mario was assured and cultured, tall and handsome, Albert seemed ill at ease, unrefined, short, and certainly could never be considered handsome.

He had left the cutter and horse tied up in the yard of the tenement house. Mabs had no idea how far it would be to the farm in Renfrew County, but she thought it would probably be an all-day ride.

The ceremony was short and without any sense of reverence or feeling. Albert and Mabel went through it as if they were stand-ins for someone else. There was to be no reception or any indication that a wedding had just taken place. When they arrived back at the house, Albert readied the cutter. He had placed bricks on the back of the Lapointe kitchen stove and these he wrapped in many layers of the *Ottawa Journal* and placed them on the floor of the cutter. The fur robe and blankets had been thrown on a heap on the kitchen floor to absorb whatever heat there was in the house. Everyone moved quickly so as not to lose the warmth any sooner than necessary. Mabs had wrapped Mary in a heavy wool blanket and she climbed in the cutter and Albert lifted Emerson in beside her. He was bundled up like a mummy which he thought was great sport, and he appeared to be the only one who was considering this new venture a happy occasion.

Mabs waved a heavily covered arm to John, Albert slapped the reins on the horse's flanks and the cutter slid over the snow-covered street, heading out of Ottawa.

There was little talk. Mabs asked about the farm. Albert, short on descriptive talents, finally ended the questions by saying "you'll see all that when we get there."

No one bothered to tell Mabel that it would be impossible to make the trip from Renfrew to the farm in the time left in the day. When they reached the town of Arnprior, which Mabs was sure was hundreds of miles from Ottawa, it was already dark. Albert pulled the cutter up in front of a neat brick house, and for a fleeting moment Mabel hoped against hope that was to be their new home. However, it turned out to belong to a cousin of Albert's who was offering overnight accommodations to cut the trip in half.

Nellie and Henry Wagonblass welcomed Mabs and the children with warmth and kindness. Nellie, childless herself, cooed to the baby, and settled her into a small pale-green spool bed, putting pillows on either side of her so she wouldn't roll off, which would have been difficult to begin with because Mary was barely six weeks old. The house was warm and cozy, and the hot supper was Mabs' first introduction to German food, which she would have to get used to if she was going to adjust to living with a German husband. She had never tasted sauerkraut before, and the blood pudding made her stomach flip-flop, but Nellie Wagonblass, sensing Mabs' uneasiness, brought out cold sliced pork from the pantry and added it to an already abundant table. Henry had started a fire in the fireplace, and as the adults sat in easy chairs in the parlour, Mabs looked around her and felt a sense of comfort. She was sure she had made the right decision in marrying Albert, and if the home she was going to was anything like this one in Arnprior, she would be content. Nellie spoke warmly of Albert when she and Mabs were "redding up" the kitchen, and Mabs heard Albert talk about the farm, and for the first time since she had laid eyes on her new husband, she heard him talk with interest about the subject he knew best. Mabs vowed she would try her utmost to be a good wife to this man. She would keep up her end of the bargain "come hell or high water", as Rosie used to say back in New York. With the thought of Rosie came a pang of loneliness. Mabs pushed it to the back of her mind. She wasn't sure how, or when, but she knew without a doubt that she would again see the De Silvas and her beloved New York. Some day. That dream would help keep her sane.

Chapter Twenty-Three

Albert said he was sure they would reach the farm in Northcote outside of Renfrew by late afternoon. The sun was bright when they left the Wagonblass house. Nellie had made a lunch which she wrapped in layers and layers of paper to keep it from freezing, and Albert tucked it under the heavy robes at their feet. Young Emerson continued to feel the whole experience was a game and he was one of the main players. He plied Albert with questions about the horse, what the farm was like and how come the runners on the cutter didn't sink into the snow down to the road. Albert, after they had left Arnprior far behind, hoisted Emerson up on his knee and let him take the reins. Baby Mary never stirred inside her warm cocoon, and only when Albert pulled the horse into the train station at Renfrew so that everyone could go inside and use the facilities, did the infant let everyone know it was feeding time.

Albert knew the stationmaster, and it looked as if he didn't need his permission to bring in the wrapped lunch and open it out on one of the seats. Mabs tried to make conversation, but Albert was either a man of few words, or he was too shy and nervous to do much more than nod at everything his new wife said.

He did explain that the road they were on after leaving Renfrew was called the Northcote side road. "It leads to Douglas. Hardly ever go there. Not much there to go for. We'll pass Briscoe's General Store. That's where I do most of the groceries. Once every two weeks I head into Renfrew," he said between puffing on his pipe and taking a swipe at his nose with the back of his leather mitt.

"How close are the neighbours? Is there anyone for Emerson to play with?" Mabs wanted to know. Albert rhymed off the names of several people who lived near the homestead. All the names sounded German, which, it turned out, they were. Except Briscoe. Mabs was reasonably sure that was an English or Scottish name.

The horse was kept at a steady trot along the Northcote side road. Albert pointed out Briscoe's General Store as they passed it, and pulling himself to the edge of the seat said, "just before that little hill there...that's our lane."

Mabs couldn't see a lane. The new snowfall had filled in any sign of tracks. A steel gate hung open and Queenie, without being steered, veered through the opening. She had made that turn many times. Here, the lane dipped and curved over moguls of snow-packed road, around spruce trees and clumps of low bushes. Mabs could see no end to the lane at first, but when the cutter rounded a corner and came to a small grade, she could see a curl of smoke reaching towards the greying sky. There was no sign of a house, only several log barns. But when the cutter turned into the barnyard, the house came into view. Mabs just stared in disbelief. It looked more like a small shed, or barn. Made of logs, it seemed no bigger than a hen house.

Albert pulled the cutter right up to the door, and jumped clear, lifting Emerson. He opened the door at the side of the house, plopped Emerson inside and then went back and took Mary from Mabs' arms, talking to the baby as he did so. "There, there...everything is going to be all right. Just wait and see."

Mabs climbed down from the cutter and saw that the pathway had been swept. Perhaps a neighbour had come over, she thought. She entered the house, stomach churning, and arms feeling like lead from holding the baby all the way from Arnprior.

Just inside the door stood two very young people. The boy looked only a couple of years older than Emerson; the girl, tall and thin, Mabs guessed to be about ten years of age. They stood ram-rod straight, their eyes never stirring from Mabs' face.

"This is Audrey. She's ten. Smart as a whip. Passed into senior fourth this year. Everett, say hello to your new Mama. Everett is eight." Both children stood as if they were growing out of the floor. Mabs was so thunderstruck she could only stare back. No one had bothered to tell her Albert had two children!

Emerson went up to Everett, and standing mere inches from him, walloped him in the stomach. "I learned that in New York. Someone hit me like that in the park one day, and I hit him back."

Everett never flinched. Mabs grabbed Emerson and steered him to a chair. Audrey went over to a couch in the corner by the cookstove and unwrapped the baby from the heavy blankets. She got on her knees and stroked Mary's hand and, turning to Mabs, asked, "Can I look after the baby? Is it a girl or a boy? I hope it is a girl. I've always wanted a baby sister. Mama died having a baby, you know." No. Mabs didn't know.

Albert wasn't privy to the dialogue in the kitchen. He had unloaded the few suitcases from the cutter and had taken the horse to the stable.

Mabs, with her heavy coat still on, looked around the room. It was getting dark and she couldn't find a light switch.

"Could we turn on a light, Everett?" Everett stood perfectly still. It was only then she realized there was no electricity. Within the hour she would learn there was also no running water, no bathroom and no telephone.

She fingered her rosary in her pocket. "Dear God in heaven. What have I done?"

Chapter Twenty-Four

Like every other rural community in the country, the telephone operator, known simply as "Central", was the human thread that held the farm people together. At Northcote, Myrtle knew everything about everyone often before they themselves knew it. That cold January it didn't take Myrtle long to advise people of the arrival of the new woman in Albert Haneman's house. Although Myrtle had never seen Mabel, she nonetheless described her right down to the colour of her hair and her genuine leather gloves. Myrtle's informant was her brother-in-law, who just happened to be the stationmaster in Renfrew where Albert and Mabel had stopped to have their lunch the previous day.

The news spread like fire through a pile of dried brush. The first to arrive at the old log house was Bertha Thom, whose house Mabs could see across the twenty-acre field that separated the two farms. She came with homemade bread and a jar of mustard pickles.

Mabs liked her immediately. She spoke in soft guttural tones which Mabs was to learn was the way most of her German neighbours spoke. Bertha had a big family, and her husband Alec's people, like Albert's she said, had come out from Germany three generations ago.

One by one neighbours from up and down the Northcote side road came to call. By the end of the week, Mabs was sure she had met more people than she ever knew back in New York! For reasons Mabs was never able to figure out, Albert would address his new wife by no other name than Mabel, and so once again she was saddled with the name she had hated from the time she was a little girl. However, she felt that in the larger scheme of things the name she was called was of little importance. Far more important was how Mabel was ever going to adjust to the transition from New York City, with the lights of Broadway virtually at her back door, department stores that ran a full city block, all the modern amenities of the era, to a drafty log house, with not so much as a bathroom.

There were two rooms upstairs and a hall almost as big as a bedroom. The slanted ceilings and walls were painted with whitewash, and the first time Mabel went upstairs she saw hoarfrost running the full length of the boards in the roof overhead. A black stovepipe snaked through the rooms and offered the only heat to the entire upstairs. Small mounds of snow sat on the only two windows in the tiny rooms, blown in where the sashes failed to meet the frames.

Downstairs, the largest room was the kitchen. It was crowded with an old couch, a huge Findlay Oval cookstove, a long pine table with two benches on either side, a high back-to-the-wall cupboard, a woodbox beside the back door, a rocking chair, a long bench at the back door where sat a wash basin under a rolled Huck towel on a wood dowel, and a table under a window that held dishes, pots, pans and jars of staples like flour and sugar. There was no sink and no icebox. At one end of the kitchen a door opened into a small room used as a parlour, whose main attraction was a set of stairs that took up more than half the room. At the other end was another bedroom and beside its door a second flight of stairs leading to the top floor. Mabs thought the house must have been built by some jack-knife carpenter who was more adept at putting up fences and repairing cow byres. The bathroom was nothing more than an outside hut, sitting in a small cluster of trees and not a stone's throw from the summer kitchen door. The summer kitchen held nothing more than row on row of cut wood to feed the Findlay Oval.

In the daytime, Mabs was in a better frame of mind. The sun poured into the big kitchen, augmenting the heat from the cookstove. She could look out the window and see Bertha's house, and the rolling hills to the west. The comforting sound of the trains as they cut through the farm beside the Bonnechere River was a connecting link to the outside world.

But when the sun went down, and night closed in around the old log house, Mabs felt like a caged animal. Audrey, anxious to please her new mother, took to looking after the baby, and each night lovingly tucked her into the crib her father had rescued from a loft over the drive shed. Emerson and Everett became fast friends although they were almost three years apart in age. Everett didn't seem to mind Emerson's pranks, which ran the gamut from hiding food he didn't like under the mattress of the bed they shared, to siccing the dog on the old gander in the barnyard. Albert, for his part, carried on as if taking a new wife was an everyday occurrence. He rose before the sun was up, lit the cookstove, did the chores, came in for breakfast and headed out again, not to be seen until dinner. Dinner, he told Mabel, not unkindly, was at noon hour. "What we eat at night, we call supper."

At first Mabel ran out of food before the meal was half over. She soon learned that Albert's appetite didn't match his stature. He liked fried potatoes, salt pork and eggs, and a heaping bowl of porridge for his breakfast. Dinner was roast beef or chicken, whipped potatoes, vegetables from the sandbin in the cellar, a couple of slices of bread, and a fruit nappy of preserves for dessert. Supper was a lighter version of dinner. Mabel eventually learned what amounts to cook and with Bertha's help was soon baking bread and sticky buns.

It became apparent that Albert had no intention of interfering with the running of the house. That's what Mabel was there for. At first she made lists for staples and Albert fetched them from Renfrew or Briscoe's General Store. But before February was half over, Mabel was hitching up the cutter and Queenie and making the twelve-mile trek into Renfrew herself.

More and more Mabel took an aggressive role on the farm. She suggested changes in the house, and though she never knew if it was Albert's desire to please or if he just wasn't the kind to argue, he willingly did just about anything he was asked to do. It was Mabel who disciplined the children and made them behave, and within a month of her arrival, both Audrey and Everett were calling her "Mother".

Albert doted on Mary. He hummed to her and sang softly in German, little ditties he had learned as a child. Apart from his pipe, which hung limp from his mouth every waking hour, Mary seemed to be his only joy. No one could say he was sullen or bad-tempered, only that Albert Haneman was a man of few words. His contentment came from working the land, from the livestock and from the homestead where he was born.

No two people could be more opposite. And although it was necessity on both their parts that had brought them together, it was a mutual respect for each other's situation that helped them adjust to living together as husband and wife. As for Albert, he had found in Mabel someone who would care for and nurture his children. For the first time since his wife had died, he felt at ease and content.

And Mabel had found a home for her two little children. But in those first few weeks on the Northcote farm Mabel felt as if she were smothering. Especially at night. When the coal oil lamps barely gave off enough light to see the corners of the room, and the wind howled outside like some deranged animal, Mabel would say silent prayers asking her God to help her get through whatever lay ahead. From the day she first laid eyes on the farm, she prayed that some way, somehow, she would be able to escape it. Had she ever known that it would take more than a decade and a tragic war before her dream would be realized, there is a very good chance Mabel would have donned her winter coat and galoshes then and there, and toting her two children in her arms, headed out into the dead of winter to recapture the life she had left behind.

Chapter Twenty-Five

Winter dragged on. Like the slow-moving hands on a clock, one bleak cold day blended in with another. The kitchen was the only room in the house that was warm enough to suit Mabel. Sometimes it was too hot, regardless of what the weather was like outside. When Albert got the fire raging in the morning, and Mabel was waiting for the oven to heat up for the day's baking, the heat bounced off the walls and blistered the wainscotting behind the stove. But if she went into another room or upstairs, the cold air met her in the face and it felt as if she were outside. Bertha showed her how to make felt slippers and blanket stitch around the edges with bright-coloured wool to hold the tops and bottoms together. Everyone in the house, including Albert, wore them at night to keep their feet warm against the drafty floors.

February gave way to March. Mary was three months old and she spent most of the time sleeping in the kitchen where Albert had made a sort of cot in the corner of the room, close to the stove. She was a contented baby, and Emerson had gotten over his jealousy of her and decided they should probably keep her after all.

"Spring is on the way," Mabel offered one morning, as the early sun beat in through the kitchen window and danced on the oil-cloth-covered floor. Mabel thought privately it was just about the ugliest piece of flooring she had ever laid eyes on.

"Don't be too sure," Albert said, draining the last of his boiled green tea, which he insisted kept him in good health. "There was a hazy ring around the moon last night. I wouldn't be surprised if it snowed again, and maybe even rained, and then watch out! It's still cold enough to freeze. An ice storm this time of year is usually a doozy."

Albert was right. Snow came silently through the night, and by mid-day had turned to sleet. The temperatures dipped and ice formed on the walkways to the pump, the barns and the driveshed. Mabel had forgotten how savage a winter could be after being in New York for so long. She pictured the trees starting to bud in Central park, and the flowers she had planted behind the house would be coming up. She was again filled with longing for what she had left behind. Alec Thom came over around mid-day to say that Briscoe's General Store had had a phone call for Mabel. No, he didn't know who it was from. "But I'll run you over to the store in the car. It's too treacherous for the horses."

Mabel bundled up, filled with anticipation. Perhaps it was Rosie. She had sent her Briscoe's number and, knowing Rosie, she was apt to phone her any time the spirit moved her. Mabel took her purse. Might as well buy the few things she needed while she was there. They skittered and slid out the lane and onto the Northcote side road.

She never knew how to take Mr. Briscoe. He was a serious but kindly man, who had little time for small talk. He handed Mabel the slip of paper with the number on it she was to call. It was Papa's number in Ottawa. Papa had never phoned her since she moved to the farm. He had written a couple of times, always including a dollar bill in the envelope.

Myrtle put Mabel through to the number, and John Lapointe answered immediately. His voice was choked with emotion, and without any preamble he got right to the reason for his call. "I have very sad news, Mabel. Your brother Henry was drowned today out at the farm in Richmond. As far as I can figure out…" He paused ever so long and Mabel thought they had perhaps lost the connection. "Papa, Papa, are you there? What happened? My God, how could Henry drown in the dead of winter?"

John Lapointe went on, labouring over his words and obviously trying desperately to keep the anguish out of his voice. "It was at the well. There is a windmill over the well, and as far as I can figure out he and young Earl were trying to get water. The platform was glare ice, and apparently Henry had taken the boards up to fix one of them. He slipped and fell into the well. By the time Earl got help, it was too late." John Lapointe broke down at that point and couldn't continue. Mabel was beyond speaking. The last time she had seen Henry, he had come to see her and the new baby at the Grace Hospital. Now he was dead, and his wife was dying in the Ottawa Sanatorium, leaving a young son virtually without parents.

Alec Thom knew his neighbour was in terrible distress. He helped her outside again and by the time they had reached the homestead, he had insisted on driving Mabel and Albert to Ottawa where the funeral was to be held. The car, he said, would be safer than trying to navigate the horses over the ice.

That night Mabel was in a state of shock. Young Henry gone. She sat in the rocking chair in the quiet kitchen. Albert had pulled supper together, and Audrey had "redded up" the kichen and put the baby down for the night. Everett and Emerson, aware of the grief, sat at the kitchen table, Emerson with his drawings and Everett quietly whittling a new slingshot.

"We'll have to take Earl, you know," Mabel said to Albert. He said neither yes or no. Whatever Mabel decided to do would suit him. Audrey heard her stepmother's comment as she was coming downstairs. "But Mother, how can we? There will be no room. Emerson and Everett are in the only double bed upstairs, and I am already sharing my room with Mary. What will we do?"

Mabel looked at Audrey for the longest moment. "What will we do? We'll find a bed. And then, all we'll do, is set another place at the table."

Chapter Twenty-Six

The day Henry was buried, word came to John Lapointe that Henry's young wife had died at the Royal Ottawa Sanatorium. The nurse who called said it was the shock of the news of her husband's accident, and the stress of wondering what was going to happen to her son, that had finally brought death to the young mother who had been ill almost since Earl's birth. She died before she learned that Henry's sister Mabel would be taking Earl to the farm in Renfrew County.

Earl came out to the farm bearing everything he owned in a small valise. He was a year older than Emerson, but much smaller in size. He had almost transparent skin, enormous black eyes and straight black hair. His face bore a strong resemblance to his father's, but he was slight of build, not at all like the rest of the Lapointes, who were tall and full of figure. He looked delicate, and Mabel made up her mind as soon as she saw him that she would take him into Renfrew to old Dr. Murphy to see if he needed a tonic.

He was painfully shy. A cot had been rolled into the back bedroom so that he could share the room with Everett and Emerson, who had been amply warned by their mother that there was to be no teasing, and that they were to make their young cousin feel welcome. That was easier said than done. Even though he had lived most of his young life on a farm with his father, it was hard to get him to leave the house. He preferred to be close to Mabel, who was sure he would be fine once he went off to school with the other children.

However, it took many months before Earl felt he belonged. Emerson and Everett taught him how to whittle slingshots and shoot tin cans off a fence post. He finally settled in at the Northcote school, and the kindly Miss Crosby, well aware of the circumstances that had brought him to Renfrew County, paid special attention to him. Before long he had caught up with the other children in his class.

Before the year was out, Earl was calling Mabel and Albert Mother and Father, and occasionally getting into mischief just like Emerson and Everett. It's a good sign, Mabel thought to herself. She was relieved.

The Haneman familty couldn't have been more diversified. Mabel, stately, with a worldly air about her, used to the finer things in life in a big cosmopolitan city; Albert, simple, plodding and content to never go much beyond Renfrew County; Audrey, forced to be grown up before her time and not that much younger than the stepmother who had come into the old log house to take over; Everett, quiet, serious and as blond as a lily; Emerson, rambunctious, mischievous, with a shock of flaming red hair; Earl, pensive, fair of skin, and just a wisp of a lad; and Mary, the baby, already starting to look like Emerson, and for the most part content to lie in her handmade crib or crawl around on the floor playing with the few toys Albert was able to build from bits and pieces of wood and empty spools of thread. This then was the Haneman household, all crammed into a small log house, originally built for half that many people. When all the children were bedded down at night, Mabel would sit at the kitchen table writing in her diaries in the dim light of the coal oil lamp. She wrote of the loneliness on the farm, the hard work that faced her every waking hour, how one day stretched into the next, all the same and with a monotony that was stifling. She knew, too, there was no escape. Albert, kind and pliant, accepted that Mabel would make most of the decisions. And so she fell into the role of head of the house, not unwillingly, but with the knowledge that it was up to her to see that the five children in her care would have the best life she could possibly give them, with the few resources she had at hand.

It was during a visit from another German neighbour that Mabel learned about egg money. Mrs. Beam was an enormous woman whom everyone called on when they were not sick enough to warrant a visit from the doctor in Renfrew twelve miles away. She had a cure for everything, and even delivered babies when the expectant mother was too busy to go into the town hospital.

Mrs. Beam was sitting at the old pine table in Mabel's kitchen. Her lisle stockings were rolled with tight elastics just below her knees, and her ample body was spread over two kitchen chairs put together. She had straight hair parted in the middle, the colour of steel wires, and held in place with two enormous grey bobby pins. Winter and summer, the perspiration poured off her face, and she kept an end of a bleached flour bag tucked down the front of her dress to mop her brow every few minutes.

"There never seems to be enough money for anything more than the bare essentials," Mabel said while she poured Mrs. Beam a cup of tea. Mrs. Beam nodded her head in agreement. "Well, I don't know what I would do without my egg money. See this dress? Bought this material at Walker's Store out of my egg money. Now, egg money doesn't only come from eggs, you know. Whatever we sell –butter, sticky buns, eggs, chickens—we call it egg money. And it's ours to keep and do with what we want. Charlie—that's my husband, you know—sometimes borrows from my egg money, but I always make him put it back." Mrs. Beam threw her head back and laughed. "Sometimes it takes him a couple months, but he puts it back, let me tell you."

Egg money. Mabel had never heard of it, but if that's what the women of Northcote did, then she would do it too. After

Mrs. Beam left, Mabel went to the back-to-the-wall cupboard and took down the big blue sugar bowl. It was never used...too big for the table. She blew the dust out of it, and put it on the bottom shelf with the cups and saucers. "This will be perfect for my egg money," she said, patting its fat side. "I won't use it for anything foolish. I'll save every cent I can, and maybe someday I will have enough to go back to visit Rosie in New York." The thought warmed her through and through, and for the first time since she moved to Northcote, she felt a hope rise in her heart. It was a hope that would take her from one day to the next, and make life, for the first time in months, bearable.

Henry Lapointe, Mabel's youngest brother and Earl's father

Albert Ernest Haneman circa 1930

Above, below, and facing page, Life on the Haneman farm

John Lapointe on a visit to Renfrew County

A Sunday family gathering. Standing, from left, Mabel's first cousin Evelyn DeGray, Mabel, Albert, Aunt Vanetta, brother Lou Lapointe, and cousin Lillian and her husband Dick Schumann; children in foreground, from left, Everett, Earl, Audrey, Emerson and Mary (with head turned)

Nellie Wagonblass (right) with her mother Rosanne Prensler

By the kitchen window, from left, Audrey, Mary, Earl, Emerson and Everett

Portrait of a young
Mary Haneman

Good friends and neighbours Bertha and Alec Thom on their way to Renfrew Fair. A young Leo can be seen in the window of the Thoms' 1930 Plymouth.

At back, from left, Audrey holding cousin Ronny, cousin Terry, Mary and Mabel. In foreground, Grandpa John Lapointe, Earl, Emerson and Albert.

Chapter Twenty-Seven

Mabel felt it wasn't right to stash all the money she made from selling her wares into the blue sugar bowl in the cupboard, so she would use some of it to help buy staples for the house, and then take the remainder and plop it into the sugar bowl.

She found many ways to make a few dollars. She baked sticky buns by the dozens (these were in great demand in the "better part" of Renfrew), and raised chickens so that she would have hens to lay eggs which she traded for staples like sugar and flour. She was always sure to keep a couple of dozen back so that she could sell them for cash, a portion of which she would tuck away in the blue sugar bowl. Fresh chickens were always in demand, and there was hardly a Saturday that Mabel didn't have the back of the buggy lined with a white sheet, upon which were laid out several newly plucked fowl.

And she watched the sugar bowl's innards grow. The contents became known as "Mother's going back to New York money". Albert thought the whole idea was sheer nonsense, but he had long since learned once his wife got an idea into her head, it was best to leave her alone with it; his chances of changing her mind were just about nil!

The couple had fallen into a gentle acceptance of each other's differences. Outsiders would say how at odds they were, both in their thinking and their background. The truth was, however, that

Mabel and Albert developed a genuine fondness for each other, and a respect for each other's diversities. Mabel greatly admired Albert's honesty, his hardworking lifestyle, and his easygoing manner. Albert was proud of Mabel's demeanour and of the way heads turned when she walked the streets of Renfrew. She had turned into a good strong farmer's wife and helper, and she was devoted to all the children, not only those she had delivered into the world. The relationship was developing into one of mutual respect, albeit without the passion either had known in their first marriages.

The twenties gave way to the thirties, and with the thirties came the Depression. The Hanemans had been poor before, scraping and scrimping to make ends meet, but with this new era came poverty such as Mabel had never known. New clothes were almost unheard of, for her or Albert, or for the children.

Mabel learned how to bleach flour and sugar bags, and lay them out on the grass in the sun to bleach out the markings. Then she would make blouses for Audrey and underwear for Mary. Some were cut into oblong pieces and embroidered at both ends for tea towels, pillow cases and small tablecloths. Others were opened flat and sewn together to make sheets. Clothes were handed down from the oldest to the youngest, with young Mary often wearing boy's shoes if a pair survived the wear and tear from one of the brothers.

Albert's sister Lizzie, who was well off (her husband Jack worked for the CPR), would gather together all her outgrown sons' clothes, pack them into a large wooden crate that had once held bulk tea, and send it off by train to Renfrew from her home in Regina. The hand-me-down box came about twice a year, and included only boys' clothes, so Mary and Audrey failed to get excited over its arrival.

Always there was a man's suit or two. Navy blue and good serge with a lot of wear in them yet. Mabel would carefully take them apart, press them with a damp tea towel on the outside, and make breeks for the boys or jumpers for the girls. An old Singer treadle machine sat in a corner of the kitchen; it had been there when Mabel arrived. Her experience on a sewing machine at Rosie's house in New York, unsuccessful as it was, gave her the courage to tackle the hand-me-down box, and there was hardly a piece of clothing in the big wooden tea box that wasn't put to good use by the time Mabel was finished with it.

Just after Mary's fifth birthday, Mabel packed a sandwich for her in a brown paper bag and sent her off to school with Audrey and the boys. There was no need to get permission from a school board, or the teacher. The child simply arrived and it was up to the teacher to work her into the one-room schoolhouse.

For the first time in five years, Mabel had the house to herself in the daytime. She would rise early in the morning, pack lunches and check behind ears and in noses, and stand at the kitchen window until the five bodies had faded from view up the long winding lane to the Northcote side road.

After she had washed on Mondays, ironed on Tuesdays, mended and sewn on Wednesdays, and baked on Thursdays and Fridays to get ready for her peddling in Renfrew on Saturdays, she would have scant time to sit and reflect on anything other than what she would serve up for supper that night. When Mabel did find a few minutes to herself, she would hoist herself into the wooden swing in the grape arbour outside, with her diaries spread around her. Sometimes she would just read them over and over again. But she never failed to write her thoughts and dreams daily into the big shiny black-covered scribblers with the rough lined paper inside. If she had no time during the day, she wrote at night.

Her diaries were forbidden territory for anyone in the household. Everyone knew that, and abided by the unspoken rule. The books came from Ritza's Rexall Drug Store where twice a year was held a One Cent Sale. For a quarter Mabel could buy five big scribblers, and for an extra nickel, get five more. And so the pile of diaries grew. Mabel insisted the children keep diaries too. She didn't care how much or what they wrote, but every night, just like saying their prayers at their mother's knee before they went to bed, they had to write entries in their diaries.

At a very young age, when she was still only printing, Mary wrote page after page, mostly about her nemesis at the Northcote school who became known as "Bad Marguerite". Emerson, who had grown into a force to be reckoned with, usually wrote one-liners like "it rained today." Mabel's diaries were kept in a drawer in a chifferobe in her bedroom. The children kept theirs stacked on the cupboard in the kitchen ready for the nightly ritual.

Mabel wrote mostly about her thoughts and sometimes she wrote short poems which said more about her feelings than any long prose:

What is this new abode
Wherein I find myself so suddenly?
With spaces as wide as the city I left behind.
I look across the fields and the hills,
And wonder why I am here.
And then I see the lives who reach out for my hand.
And my answer comes
As surely as the blossoms on the vine.

It was a damp, bleak day on the farm in Northcote. Rain hovered overhead, but failed to show by noon hour. The children left in well-worn raincoats and were told to take their shoes off for the trek home if it was raining. Better to have wet feet than ruined running shoes. It was mid-summer, and the humidity hung around the old log house like unseen clouds. Mabel had taken to buying the *Philadelphia Enquirer* every Saturday out of her egg money. She spread the latest edition out on the old pine table in the kitchen. The section on New York was always the first page Mabel read. Her brother Louis wrote scant letters of the city she had left behind, where he had risen to a senior position in a marble company. His letters weren't enough to satisfy Mabel's curiosity about her beloved city, and the *Philadelphia Enquirer* was her final link to what she had given up and left behind.

As always, she cut out pieces of news for her scrapbooks. For reasons she would never be able to explain later, that day she put her head down on the table and wept. Her tears dampened the newspaper, and left her weak and despondent.

She looked around the room. She had been on the farm seven years, and apart from new flour-bag curtains on the windows, a new dishpan, and the stove pipes painted silver, nothing had changed. Mabel was still a young woman. "How many years can I endure this isolation?" she asked herself. "My God, if I have to stay here until I am old and grey I will surely die before my time. Not of illness, but of sheer loneliness and despair." Mabel craved the opera, Broadway, the elevated trains, yes, even the Automat with its ten-cent meals.

It was as if Mabel had become two people. She was a devoted homemaker, and took pride in her children and her newly learned abilities in the kitchen. She worked in the Lutheran church, helped neighbours at thrashing time, and baked for Old Herman, the bachelor who lived on the next line. Her days were full.

But this terrible longing for what she had once known was never far from the surface of her feelings. She watched Albert toil from morning to night, coming in for his supper bone tired, and with little energy to do much more than read the *Ottawa Farm Journal* before falling into bed in his long underwear, often still wearing his work socks.

Mabel no longer compared Albert with Mario. That was a fruitless exercise. But what she saw was a man who was wearing out. Although he denied it, Albert was weary. His only enjoyment was driving into town on a Saturday night, and sitting around the office at Thacker's Garage while his wife and children "did the main street".

The old Model T Ford Albert had gotten by trading many loads of gravel from his pit looked as if it was held together with hairpins. It was impossible to get as far as Renfrew without experiencing several flat tires, and the crank, more than once, sent his arm into a tailspin as the motor backfired on starting. But to Albert the car was a step up from the horse and buggy. To Mabel, it was a symbol of what their life had become—bartering to survive, backbreaking work, and uncertainty about the future. There had to be some way to escape, and that day at the kitchen table, with the Philadelphia paper spread out before her, and her tears flowing like water from the pump in the yard, Mabel prayed for a way out. She knew in her heart Albert would be happier in a town where he could perhaps get a job suited to his capabilities, and Mabel could buy one of those Arborite tables she saw in Mrs. Stewart's kitchen when she delivered eggs on Saturday mornings. Yes, an Arborite table...grey, with a shiny piece of ribbed steel running all around its edges. And if all went well, they could trade in the old Model T, and maybe buy a Huppmobile. She had seen one parked in Dr. Murphy's driveway the week before.

Mabel fantasized that day, letting her mind caress her thoughts, giving herself courage. If she had a goal, then she could work towards it. She wouldn't share her dream. She'd write about it, but she wouldn't tell anyone. Not even Rosie in New York. She tingled all over as she mentally tried to decide what town they could move to. It needn't be a grand house, but it certainly wouldn't be log. A new table and a new car. Those would be the ultimate goals when they moved off the farm.

Chapter Twenty-Eight

The silent dream of escaping the farm was never far from Mabel's mind. How she would accomplish this, she wasn't sure. Albert would be hard to convince the move would be for the better. He had been born in the old log house, and apart from trips into Ottawa and one or two trips to Montreal, he had never ventured out of Renfrew County. Farming was his life. He knew no other. He was the third generation of Haneman to live on the parcel of land at Northcote. Mabel knew all this, but so convinced was she that they would have a better life in a town, that she hung onto her dream, and was sure that when the right moment presented itself, she would be able to convince Albert that moving off the farm would be the best thing that could ever happen to the family.

And so the years passed, slowly and not without hardship. The Depression was at its peak. But it was a poor farmer indeed who could not keep food on his table. The smokehouse was always full of meat; there were vegetables in the sandbins in the cellar. Each fall two big barrels, one of sauerkraut and one of salt pork were filled and rolled into the summer kitchen to be used all winter. The hens were good layers and a small orchard supplied enough apples to last well into early Spring. There was just no money. No money for anything but the bare essentials.

The DeGrays, Mabel's aunt and uncle who lived in the middle apartment in the tenement house in Ottawa, came out to the farm regularly, and left with the car full of meat and vegetables and jars of pickles and preserves. "Poor as church mice," Mabel would say, as the entire family waved them goodbye when they left the yard. "At least we have food for our stomachs," and she would sigh with what was almost a sound of contentment.

Herby, Mabel's brother from Montreal, took to sending his two young boys to the farm every summer. Ronny and Terry often stayed and attended the Northcote school in September. Ronny, the older of the two young brothers, and close to Mary's age, was a handful, and Albert was sure he was going straight to reform school when he grew up. "If he ever grows up," he would add, shaking his head and blowing rings of pipe smoke into the air.

Terry was curly haired and angelic. The two brothers couldn't have been more different. And Mabel loved having them at the farm. They helped fill the void in her life that grew each year. In fact, company was one of the saving graces for Mabel. Even Albert's sister Lizzie from Regina who came once a year, and who according to Albert put on such airs as to be a "real pain in the neck", at least gave Mabel something to look forward to.

But the visits from her brother Louis from New York City were what she really craved. Often he came without notice, so Mabel was in a perpetual state of readiness. "Lou might be coming this week. Haven't heard from him for a while. That's always a good sign. Wouldn't be a bit surprised if he drove in the yard tomorrow," she would say, looking out the lane wistfully.

When Lou did come, he brought New York newspapers, fresh fruit picked up in Renfrew on his way to the farm and suitcases full of gifts for everyone. He drove a big black Buick with an enormous gold eagle on the hood of the car, and wore grey flannel shirts and well pressed pants. He was the picture of success, which of course he was. He had taken over a marble company and had worked on the Waldorf Astoria and the Empire State Building, bringing little pieces of tile to the children in Renfrew County to prove it. Mabel was very proud of Lou.

While he was visiting, there were trips into Renfrew to the fair, evenings at the picture show, and singsongs before bedtime, when he and Mabel would sing in harmony. Although no one ever admitted it, it was through Lou's generosity that the Hanemans were finally able to afford a telephone.

Mabel's other brother Amby, married with five children and living in St. Catharines, came less frequently. But whenever any of the brothers came to visit, John Lapointe would drive out from Ottawa and there would be great laughing and singing and step dancing, and everyone would sleep wherever he could find a place to lay down his head. Children would sleep crossways in the beds, and in the summertime Albert would pitch the big tent and the overflow from the little log house would bed down under the grape arbour. The visits would give Mabel a reprieve from her loneliness, and only when the house was quiet again would she slip back into her melancholy, and privately dream and plan for the day when they could bid goodbye to the farm.

Within the first year of being on the farm, Mabel had given up trying to keep in touch with Mario's family in New York. Her letters went unanswered. They had been adamantly opposed to Mabel's coming back to Canada, even for a visit. And when she wrote that she had remarried and stressed in the letter that she took the step to make a home for Mario's two children, she still heard nothing in reply. After many months, she gave up trying to keep the relationship alive. Her friendship with Rosie and Raine, however, continued, marred only by the distance that separated them physically. The De Silvas now had three children, and Raine had opened his own practice. According to Rosie, he "was blessed in having both Jewish and Spanish patients to keep him busy." Both Mabel and Rosie talked about the day when one or the other would visit, and Mabel told Rosie in her letters about the blue sugar bowl and how it grew weekly. What she didn't tell her was how it took one step forward and two steps backward, as Albert would dip into it for a new inner tube for the car, or a piece of harness, or some other emergency for which there was no money. And even though the Depression was supposed to be universal, it was obvious to Mabel that Rosie lived a good life with all the amenities offered by a big city, while she struggled each day to make ends meet, and never went to bed without praying for the courage and the strength to face the next day.

Chapter Twenty-Nine

Mabel knew that timing was everything when it came to talking to Albert about moving off the farm. It wasn't an idea he was going to accept willingly. And in the meantime, Mable would continue to go on as before. She had made many friends throughout the community. Many people were in awe of her. Her once thin body had filled out considerably, In fact, she lamented about the weight she had put on, and blamed it on the big meals and the rich dishes that were standard fare on the farm. Albert teased her too. He always ate as if it were his very last meal on earth and failed to gain an ounce. Mabel, on the other hand, after about eight years on the farm, got to look more and more like the rest of the Lapointe family—tall, full of body and face, and still retaining the dark good looks her remaining brothers had inherited from John Lapointe. Stately. That's what people in Renfrew called her.

Mabel took every opportunity to expose her children to the finer things of life. There were many opportunities available to children in Renfrew that her children were deprived of simply because they lived in the country. And so she fought for library cards, when the town library much preferred to issue them only to those who lived within the town limits. "Discrimination. Plain and simple discrimination," Mabel hissed to the stern librarian, who reluctantly filled out five white cards and laid down rules over and above what she expected from Renfrew member children. "Only one book each. And they must be back here every Saturday. And if there is a mark on them, they will have to be replaced." Mabel accepted the rules and followed every one of them, so determined was she that her children should have the advantage of belonging to the town library.

She scanned the *Renfrew Mercury* every week to see what events were being held that the five Haneman children might take advantage of. They went to displays, concerts and plays usually available only to those children who lived within the town limits.

In the dead of winter, she even bundled them up and took them into Renfrew to sing on a street corner with the Salvation Army band, which Albert thought was just as crazy an idea as he had ever heard of. "I'll wait for you at Thacker's Garage," he'd say. "And remember, we're Lutherans. No one is joining the Salvation Army, and that's final."

Mabel badgered the officials until her three boys were allowed to play on the town softball team. "I go into Renfrew every Saturday anyway, the boys might as well come too." And so everyone would rise at sunup, do the chores, eat a hearty breakfast and load themselves into the Model T, which Mabel now drove like a maniac down the washboard road leading to the highway. They would play on the team, wearing a mish-mash of uniforms obtained by trading chickens and vegetables with a woman whose sons no longer played ball. Mabel couldn't afford the proper shoes, and for a time the coach was reluctant to let them play in high-top running shoes, but Mabel intervened and said if they could run like the wind in the shoes they owned what did it matter? And so the three farm boys played ball for several summers. Mabel was pleased they could hold their own, as she had known they would.

Mabel had always been very musical, and it wasn't long after she moved to the farm in Renfrew County that she mastered the harmonica. She learned on a 50-cent model that came in a grab-bag from Ritza's Rexall Drug Store, and later she took a giant step up to a two-dollar model. She could play anything on it. She played at the Saturday night house parties which were common throughout the community, keeping up with Alec Thom on his fiddle. And she taught young Mary to step dance and do the highland fling, in spite of having no previous knowledge of either. Mary was soon dancing all over the county at Christmas concerts and church events. Albert was very proud of both of them.

From all outward appearances, it seemed that Mabel had settled into a routine of contentment on the farm. But the children knew there was a restlessness in her. Especially Audry, who was so much older than the others. She often found her stepmother stretched out on the grass in the backyard, close to the wheatfield, doing nothing more than watching the white clouds float by in a brilliant sky. Or Mabel would count the blackbirds, saying, "One for sorrow, Two for joy, Three for a girl, Four for a boy; Five for silver, Six for gold, Seven for a secret ne'er to be told."

Only Mabel knew what the secret was. She harboured it in her heart, not daring to share it with anyone. She would be moving off the farm. To civilization. Where houses had bathrooms and electric lights and where the children could have the advantage of better and bigger schools. But she wouldn't tell anyone. The right time would come. And when it did, she would be ready.

Chapter Thirty

Although the Depression had come to a close, there was little change on the farms in Renfrew County, or for the rest of Canada for that matter. There was no sign of better times. People still struggled to make ends meet.

Many changes had taken place out on the Haneman homestead these nine years past, and yet much had stayed the same. Audrey had finished at the Northcote School, and although the opportunities were limited in that era for girls who didn't go on to high school, she found work in the home of one of the wealthier families in Renfrew. But she was so lonesome, she only lasted a few weeks. To go into nursing or teaching she would have to go back to school, and that seemed unlikely given the times, and so Mabel encouraged her to stay at home on the farm, not only helping in the house but working outside as well. Because she was such a good worker, Mabel knew she could go back to town and get another job whenever she felt ready.

Everett, too, had finished public school. He "hired out" at day work farms in the area, but came home at night. Emerson and Earl would soon be finished school as well. Emerson showed a great talent for drawing, like his father before him, and spent hours with a pencil and pad creating buildings with glass fronts and elevators that went up on the outside. Everyone in the family thought

Emerson was a bit strange. "Imagine elevators going up on the outside of a building," Audrey would laugh. "And whoever heard of glass walls," someone else would say. Mabel said nothing, knowing in her heart that her son had inherited not only his father's talent for drawing, but his imagination as well. She was sure he would go on to higher education and make his mark in the world, just as Mario would have done had he lived.

Mary, still in the junior grades, was gangly and covered with freckles which she hated with a passion. Her hair was as red as fire, a constant concern for the young girl, who was sure if her mother would just let her dye it black like Aunt Lizzie's, she would at least be able to compete with her school nemesis Marguerite, whose blonde curls came right out of a bottle from Ritza's Rexall Drug Store.

Earl was the most serious of the five children. He had lost so much out of his life that Mabel wondered if he would ever fully recover. He too was artistic, but in a different way. He liked to carve and whittle, and would spend many hours at the back stoop with his pen-knife and a piece of wood, piling up shavings. Having long since gone past the slingshot stage, he would create little forest animals which he lined up on the windowsill in the upstairs bedroom.

Albert plodded along each day as he had done all his life. He was content to deal with the seasons as they came, never really planning much further ahead than the time slot he was in. He was considered a good farmer, but because of the lay of the land, the farm would never be prosperous. Mabel knew this. She also knew that, as the boys grew up, they would want to shape their own lives, likely away from the farm. When that happened, she reasoned, Albert would be unable to look after the farm on his own. She dreaded the time when the children would be old enough to leave, but she knew too that the day must come. And perhaps then, she could finally put into motion her plan to move away too. This plan was always just below the surface of her being. She still didn't talk about it to anyone, but she knew in her heart the day would come.

Silently, she found so much wrong with her surroundings. She hated the pine furniture. It reeked of poverty to her. She was bone tired of the monotonous routine of her day-to-day existence. She would sit for long spells at a time and reprove herself for her thoughts, but that did little to ease her restlessness. She knew she would be more content had she never known another way of life....But she couldn't change that; the other life had happened.

What she could change, perhaps, was how she and Albert and the children would spend the rest of their lives, and she prayed silently that it wouldn't be out on that farm in Renfrew County.

Albert's sister, the
fashionable "Aunt Lizzie"

Bertha and Alec
Thom and family

Above: Albert taking a noon break from chores

Below: Emerson on his Harley-Davidson "Miss Carriage" in Holland, 1944

Albert and Mabel Haneman

Chapter Thirty-One

Even the *Renfrew Mercury*, which usually paid little attention to news of the world, preferring instead to dwell on all things rural and of special interest to the farming community it served, had started to run editorials, and sometimes borrowed columns from the *Ottawa Farm Journal*, on the inevitability of war. It was 1939. The talk at Briscoe's General Store among the farmers that spring took on a tone even more serious than the recent lack of rain and how poorly the crops had done last year. "Another year like that could be disastrous," Charlie Beam said. And then the talk shifted to the prospect of war and how it was likely just about every family in the county would be affected one way or another. In the Haneman household, a gloom settled in as both Albert and Mabel realized that at least one of the boys was of enlisting age. Everett, although young in his parents' eyes, was in fact no younger than the Kallies lad who had taken the train into Ottawa to join up.

But the following year it was young Emerson who was the first to join the thousands of young Canadians who enlisted. He was only sixteen, but would soon be seventeen. Big for his age, he looked much older. He said he was going to join the Air Force. He loved planes, and at the time, was sure that as soon as he was handed a uniform, he would also be handed a licence to fly.

Within a few days of leaving Renfrew, he was back in full Air Force uniform. Mabel cried when she saw him. She said to Albert, "Emerson is little more than a boy."

But in his uniform he looked much older, with his wedged cap on the side of his head, and he showed everyone how he had been taught to hold his fingers on his forehead to get the proper angle and height for the hat. That night he shined his black boots until they were like glass. Mabel cried again.

Within the month, Everett too was on his way to enlist. He settled on the army. He said one pilot in the family was enough. He said, "With my luck, Emerson and I would end up on the same plane and that could spell trouble." He laughed at the thought of the two of them cavorting around the sky in an Air Force plane; such was the lightheartedness of the youth who went off to fight the adult war. Neither Mabel nor Albert thought Everett's attempt at humour was at all funny.

Like Emerson, Everett came home dressed in his army clothes. He was very proud that he had learned to iron his shirts in pleats. And he showed everyone that night at the supper table how he could shine the brass on his uniform by pushing a steel bar with a slit in it under the buttons to keep the polish off the material. Young Mary thought that was just about the cleverest trick she had ever seen.

Emerson barely had time to get used to his uniform when he was shipped overseas. He had joined up less than three months previously, and yet to Mabel it seemed he had been away forever. He celebrated his seventeenth birthday in Holland, and Mabel cried the whole day. She made a birthday cake for him, but none of the family felt much like eating it, and so she took it down the Northcote road to Old Herman, who was more than pleased to be celebrating Emerson's birthday.

The farm took on a certain quietness after the two older brothers left. Earl would be turning eighteen the next fall, and he complained constantly about having to do the chores of three people. He said he was going to join up as soon as the school year ended. In fact, he didn't wait until his eighteenth birthday.

Then a phone call came from Everett. He couldn't say exactly when, but he was "shipping out", as he called it. Mabel was frantic. One of those thin blue paper air-mail letters had just arrived from Emerson, who said he had been taken into someone's home in Holland for his birthday. That made Mabel cry again. Before the week was out, the family was notified that Everett had left Canada. Mabel said it wasn't right to lose two sons in less than a couple of months. Albert had to remind her that they were just away, they hadn't been lost. "Yet," was her reply. And then young Earl appeared in his army uniform. Still slight of build, with a young boy's face, he looked as if he might be dressed up as a soldier for a masquerade party.

Everett wrote, just a few lines, to say that his troop had landed safely in Italy. Audrey pulled Emerson's map book out from under his bed and opened it on the kitchen table. She found Holland and Italy, and young Mary measured them off with a ruler to try to find out how far they were apart. She said maybe the brothers could meet for Sunday supper sometime. Mabel cried again.

Earl was sent to Halifax, and he was to remain in the Maritimes for the better part of the war, which greatly relieved both Albert and Mabel, although she still threatened to write to the government to see if Canada could put an end to this senseless war that was snatching young boys right out of their homes. Of course, the letter was only in her mind. She knew very well the futility of such action.

Now there were only three to pray on the braided rug at night. Albert never did get down on his knees when Mabel gathered the children around her before bedtime. After the three boys left the farm, Audrey and Mary were subjected to longer, and what Mabel called more meaningful, praying. They prayed endlessly for the brothers' safekeeping. They prayed for an end to the war. They prayed for every young man in Renfrew County who enlisted (Audrey was grateful her mother had decided against naming all of them), and then when they came to the end of the prayers Mabel announced that it was "private prayer time". Everyone stayed in place and silently prayed and gave thanks: Audrey prayed for a good job in Renfrew, Mary prayed that Bad Marguerite would fall off the face of the earth and Mabel prayed that she would have the courage to find a way to tell Albert the time had come to leave Northcote and the farm, and go on to a better life in some town in the Ottawa Valley.

Chapter Thirty-Two

Maybe it was the power of suggestion. And maybe it really was the fact that for the first time in many years, Albert had no help on the farm, but he lamented more than once that he was finding the running of the farm alone an almost impossible load. Goodness knows Mabel had planted the idea that he was working too hard, and that as far as she could see, it was only going to get worse as he got older.

Now, Albert wasn't an old man by any means. There were many farmers in the area much older than he was. But most of them had grown boys who hadn't gone off to the war, or else they could afford hired hands. Tommy Rohr, the tramp who wandered in off the tracks one day years ago, really couldn't be called a hired hand. He worked for his room and board and a flat fifty of Player's cigarettes every Saturday. Albert knew he was worth more than that, but there just wasn't the money to pay him. Tommy had seemed content with the arrangement, at least as long as Emerson, Everett and Earl were around to share the load. But with them gone, Tommy said he thought he might move on too, and he found work at a farm on the Barr Line.

And so Albert was alone. Mabel helped all she could. She milked morning and night, but she was no good with the plough, or mending fences, and she had no stomach for slaughtering beef and pigs. Mabel's unrest, coupled with Albert's growing weariness, began to have an effect. Like water dripping for a very long time on a stone, one drop at a time, eventually starting to make a dent, so Albert's will to keep farming began to dissipate. Leaving the farm, however, was the furthest thing from his mind. He thought of share cropping with Alec Thom, or just running cattle. But the idea of quitting the homestead, to Albert, was never an option.

In that respect, he and Mabel differed entirely. Mabel could see no earthly reason to stay on a farm and not work the land. And although she never said out loud how unhappy she was, the idea of getting away from the dreariness of the old log house without even the most trifling of amenities was always in her mind.

To everyone, the onset of the Second World War was a tragedy. Early in Canada's involvement, many young men had already lost their lives. Mabel and Albert lived in dread that every time the mailman left a letter it would be from the government telling them terrible news about one of their boys. No, there was no doubt about it, the war was terrible and no one would have been happier than Mabel and Albert to see it end.

And yet, in a way, it offered Mabel her first chance of escape. The boys were gone. Albert wasn't getting any younger. Now, she finally told him, it was time to get off the farm and move to a town where he would find a good paying job, and she could perhaps put her nurses' training to use.

All their married life, Albert had been the compliant one. Even now he found it much easier to accept Mabel's proposal than oppose it. Perhaps he knew in his heart that there was nothing to hold Mabel to the farm. At any rate, a year after the boys had gone, the decision was made...mutually or otherwise...that the farm would be sold, and all that was left to decide was to which town they would move.

Chapter Thirty-Three

Getting rid of the farm wasn't nearly so difficult as both Mabel and Albert thought it would be. The long acreage, like every other farm in Northcote, ran in one long narrow strip north and south, and abutted Alec Thom's farm. Not only did he buy most of the live-stock, he bought the Haneman homestead as well. Although some of the Thoms' boys had joined the forces, there were still two strapping young teenagers at home to help out, and so taking over more tillable land did not create much more of a workload.

Mabel had decided on a small town closer to Ottawa as the site of their new home. It was out of Renfrew County, it was close to relatives in the Capital, and she was able to find a house to rent that wasn't made of logs!

Albert looked at the place with little or no interest. A house was a house as far as he was concerned. Emotionally, Albert still couldn't come to terms with the move off the homestead. While the final closing of the sale to Alec Thom took place, Albert walked from one end of the farm to the other. He climbed the West Hill, and tossed stones in the Bonnechere where he swam and fished as a young lad. He stood at the gravestones, cornered off in the field behind the barn, where his ancestors had been buried, and pulled away the long grass from the simple markers. "Augustav Haneman, born 1831, died 1888"—Albert's grandfather, who came from Germany and settled the farm, and raised three sons and two daughters. They were all long gone, and Albert could barely remember his own father's face. He wasn't in the farm plot, but had been buried at Rosebank, beside Albert's mother and Albert's first wife.

Albert wandered through the barns, and into the ice house where the remnants of last winter's ice harvest still remained buried in the sawdust. All the livestock had gone, and the out-buildings were empty. Albert went to sit in the grape arbour on the old wooden swing and wondered what he would do with the rest of his life.

Mabel was packing dishes and clothes in big boxes, and Albert couldn't hide his distress when she told him she wasn't moving one stick of furniture except a few pieces she could tolerate. He looked at the old pine table, hand-hewn by his grandfather, and the crudely made but comfortable kitchen chairs, with the rug mats on the seats. Mabel hated twig furniture with a passion, but, perhaps through sympathy for Albert, or perhaps because it was the most solid of the twig furniture, she decided one small table would be moved to be put on the verandah of the new house. As for the rest of the furniture, Mabel said if she ever laid eyes on another pine deacon's bench or a dough box as long as she lived, it would be too soon for her.

Mabel went through the house and packed two hump-backed trunks with what she called "memories". These were bits and pieces she thought her children would cherish when they were older. She attached small notes to each piece, telling of its history and why it was important to them. When the trunks were full of things like string-knit dishclothes, an ice scraper, the cream skimmer and the wood tongs for taking the clothes out of boiling water on the back of the cookstove, she locked the trunks and whacked the lock with her hand to make sure it was secure. Then she took the keys down to the river and tossed them as far as she could throw them. Her instructions to Audrey were: "These two trunks are to be opened only after I am gone. They are packed full of memories. Although these have been hard and sometimes painful years, I want you to remember them. What I have put in the trunks, with their stories, will be your only link to this farm. You are to share these memories with your brothers and sister when the right time comes."

Chapter Thirty-Four

As Renfrew county slipped further and further away, the mid-afternoon sun started to drop in the sky. There would still be plenty of daylight, and with any luck the old Model T would make it safely to the small town the Haneman family was moving to. Albert had fixed four flat tires along the way, and the rad had spewed steaming water twice, forcing more stops along the road than he had bargained for.

Mary and Audrey were restless in the back seat. The lunch was gone, and Mabel had tired of blowing out tunes on the harmonica and tucked it away in her purse. "This looks just like Northcote," Mary said. "I thought everything would be different." "It's still the Ottawa Valley, you ninny," Audrey retorted.

Albert's pipe had long since gone out. It probably needed tobacco, he thought. But it still hung loosely in his mouth. He considered stopping on the side of the road to fill the bowl, but decided the sooner they got this trip over, the better. And so the pipe stayed suspended, held in place by dry lips, and clenched between his teeth, making his jaw ache.

Audrey said she was getting chilly. Mabel told her to roll down the curtains in the back of the car. Mary lamented that if Audrey did that she wouldn't be able to see out. "Nothing to see anyway," Audrey said, poking Mary a good one in the side of her ribs.

Mabel sighed in the front seat. "Can't please everybody, I guess."

The car steamed along at a good rate for a Model T. And then after more than a half-day of driving, the town sign was before them. "Carleton Place." Mabel almost sang the words. "Isn't that a lovely name? Doesn't it sound like it has a wonderful history? I intend to learn all I can about it. And when we were here to look for a house, the people were so friendly. Remember, Albert?"

Mabel had moved to the very edge of the front seat to get a better look. There were only houses along the street leading into the town, no factories like there were in Renfrew. Many of the homes were small, and most were painted white or had red brick siding on them. Some were solid red brick, and they were larger, with sweeping verandahs, and gardens at the side.

A factory whistle in the distance blew its shrill announcement that it was the end of the workday. Mabel thought it was a lovely sound...friendly-like. "I think it's a welcome for us, don't you, Albert?" Albert said nothing, pretending to be intent on aiming the car in the right direction.

"Stop here, Albert. I want to get the feel of the town. Years from now I want to be able to remember what it was like on this day."

Albert did as he was bade. He eased the car over to the side of the street just before the railroad crossing. He looked blankly ahead, turning his head neither left nor right.

It was at that very moment in time that Mabel, after so many years of just existing day after day, began to live. Really live.

And it was that day that Albert started to die.

Epilogue

Mabel Ernestine Haneman died on Christmas morning, 1971.

Albert Ernest Haneman died in 1981.

Everett Haneman died in 1990.

Earl (Lapointe) Haneman died in 1998.

Audrey (Haneman) Bergeron, who raised 17 children, still resides in Ottawa.

Emerson Haneman lives in Port Stanley, Ontario.

Mary Haneman Cook lives in Carleton Place, Ontario.

The old farm is now owned by Alec and Bertha Thom's son Leo and his wife Ilene. The log house was sold and moved to another location. Several of the barns still stand. The site of the farm still creates much interest because of Mary's long-running CBC radio series of stories of the Depression years in Renfrew County. Several times a year busloads of people descend on the site to walk the land and view what is left of the grape arbour, the ice house and the foundation of the old log house.

A renowned storyteller, columnist and CBC radio broadcaster, **Mary Cook** has been delighting reading and listening audiences for years with her remembrances of growing up on a family farm during the bittersweet years of the 1930s. She is the recipient of seven Actra awards and is the author of seven books.

Available from Creative Bound Inc.
1-800-287-8610
(613) 831-3641

Christmas with Mary Cook is a collection of Mary's most requested yuletide stories and recipes. From Pork Tourtières and Old-Fashioned Christmas Fruitcake to "The Doll", "Letters from School", and "December Birthday", this special edition is sure to warm winter hearts everywhere. [Net proceeds from the sale of this book, now in its second edition, are donated to the Saunders-Matthey Foundation for Breast Cancer Research.]

0-921165-51-X $15.00